The New Vesta Secret

Finding the Flame of Faith, Home & Happiness

A True Story

By Debra May Macleod

© Debra May Macleod   2014
ISBN-13: 978-1503289468

All rights reserved. No part of this publication may be reproduced, stored in a retrieval system, or transmitted in any form or by any means, electronic, mechanical, photocopying, recording or otherwise, without the prior written permission of the author.

Debra May Macleod asserts the moral right to be identified as the author of this work.

The author has tried to recreate events, dates, locales and conversations from memory; however, the names and identifying characteristics of some people and places have been changed to protect identity.

Cover photo: Fire alphabet letter V © Kesu
Image ID: 110466455 Provided by Shutterstock.com

Inside illustration: Letter V logo   © Steinar
Image ID: 206140168 Provided by Shutterstock.com

NewVesta.com

CONTENTS

Introduction   The Via Sacra…..Page 6

Chapter I   Playing With Fire…..Page 18
    The Master Plan
    Conception and Denial
    Crash and Burn
    Acceptance

Chapter II   From the Ashes…..Page 27
    Scared Straight
    The Rebound
    Taking My Work Home With Me
    From Anger to Apathy
    Cold and Miserable

Chapter III   Las Vesta…..Page 39
    A Blast From the Past
    Basement Excavations
    A Risky Revelation
    The Lararium

Chapter IV   Revelations and Roots…..Page 50
    Lighting (and Lightening) Up
    Finding Our Roots
    Seeing Things in a New Light

Chapter V	Reigniting the Flamma Vesta…..Page 62
	Trial by Fire
	A Spark of Simplicity
	Catching Fire
	The Flame and the Furnace
	The Voice of New Vesta
Chapter VI	Happiness and Heaven…..Page 74
	Get Thee to a Nunnery
	Mother Vesta
	The Sacred Feminine: A Spiritual Void
	Eat, Pray, Leave
	Finding Happiness at Home
	Self-Creation
Chapter VII	Finding a Focal Point…..Page 91
	The Power of Focus
	Staying Focused
	A Face in the Flame
	Women's Intuition
Chapter VIII	Vesta, Renewed…..Page 102
	New Beginnings
	Fire Power: Cleansing and Renewing
Chapter IX	Liturgy and the Light of New Vesta…..Page 107
	Greek Tragedy
	Alpha and Omega
	Ritual and Doctrine
	Ritual and Revelation
	The Elysian Fields

                    The Eternal Flame
                    The Power of Symbols

Chapter X   Spiritual Evolution…..Page 122
                    Life's Main Intersection
                    Sparks and Superpowers
                    Sparks and Secrets

Supplement
The Five Tenets of the New Vesta Tradition…..Page 131

      Tenet One: A Household Lararium with Vestal Candle
      Tenet Two: Daily Offerings and Prayer
      Tenet Three: Ancestral Roots
      Tenet Four, Part I: Light Reflection
      Tenet Four, Part II: Light Reflection & Renewal
      Tenet Five: Wearing a New Vesta Symbol

INTRODUCTION

The Via Sacra

This is the true story of how I stumbled upon the last artefact of a banished spirituality and how its sacred flame helped me find faith and happiness at home, revere my life and loves, and renew my spirit. In all humility, I hope it may do the same for you.

- Debra May Macleod

It happened as the daylight first started to fade on March 1st, 1989. I was twenty years old, small-town all the way, and wandering – wide-eyed with culture shock and the thrill of traveling alone – among the colossal ruins of the Roman Forum. I had wings on my feet and far more life ahead of me than behind me.

Looking back, I could weep for such freedom and potential. I could, but I don't have time. There are clients to call, suppers to cook, laundry to wash, a galaxy of *Star Wars* toys to pick off the floor before the dog chews them.

The wings are still there. They're just tucked into high-heels and sheep slippers, the footwear that defines the duality of my present life. Work and family.

If you've never visited or heard of the Roman Forum, it is the ancient rectangular plaza around which the great City of Rome grew, did business and prospered. From the 8th century BCE, it was the heart of political, economic and religious life in the Roman Republic.

As such, it boasted all manner of architecture, from the simple Regia where the first kings of Rome lived to the elaborate religious temples where sacrifices were made to the Roman gods and goddesses.

During the days of the Roman Empire, the Forum's marble gleamed under the Italian sunshine as a series of famous and sometimes infamous Caesars ruled the world and made history.

Julius Caesar, who had a love affair with Cleopatra of Egypt and was stabbed twenty-three times by senators; Augustus, who ruled during the Pax Romana, the greatest period of peace Rome ever enjoyed; Tiberius, under whose reign Christ was crucified; Caligula, the madman who made his horse a senator; Commodus, the sadist who fancied himself a gladiator and vomited up the assassin's poison until those he terrorized finally strangled him in his bath.

Today, the Forum is in ruins. For many centuries, it was eaten away by time, weather, war, indifference and intolerance. Christian vandals decapitated statues of beloved pagan gods and goddesses, carved crosses in their foreheads and stripped the marble off their temples to build churches.

It wasn't until the early nineteenth century that restorations slowly began. Broken reliefs and statues, chunks of giant columns, soaring arches and remnants of towering temples started to rise again and these continue to rise amid modern excavations. Modern visitors to the Forum can now see shadows of its former grandeur and glory.

I was walking among such shadows that early spring so long ago. During my first life. The life before the husband and child and dogs and housework and obligations and exhausted evenings.

The few foreign friends I had picked up along my travels had gone off in search of food and drink and I was left alone to wander down the cobblestones of the Via Sacra, Rome's "sacred road" that led from the Capitoline Hill through the Forum and to the Colosseum.

On either side of the Via Sacra, massive columns and stones lay scattered among tall grass and bushes. It is as if, many generations ago, the Roman god Jupiter scooped every temple and structure into his colossal hands, smashed them to near bits, and then sprinkled them along the length of the ancient road.

A cool breeze blew in and blew out the few straggling tourists on the path behind me. Being Canadian, I've always been able to tolerate the cold better than I can tolerate crowds, so I was delighted to have the Roman Forum all to myself.

I took a few liberties, too, veering off the beaten path in ways that Rome's history and tourism department would not have looked kindly upon.

With a rowdy gang of feral cats as my only companions, I spent some time admiring the detailed Arch of Septimius Severus. It wasn't until one of the cats let out a particularly creepy howl that I noticed how late it was getting. I tossed the scruffy creature the last remnants of a salami sandwich I'd been carrying around since lunch, and then started to make my way out of the Forum.

Picking up the pace, I walked until I came across an elderly woman, alone, standing beside the ruins of a small white temple where a few columns still stood. She was burning a candle. I nodded a polite hello, the universal greeting of travelers, and kept walking; however, I couldn't resist a look back over my shoulder. As if knowing I'd do it, she smiled warmly and waved me over.

"*Ciao, e` tranquilla stasera.*"

"I'm sorry, I don't speak Italian," I said.

"American?"

"Canadian."

"Ah, more quiet," she laughed.

"A little," I grinned back.

"I never go Canada," she said, "but go America many times. I have *fratello*, brother, in New York. Where in Canada you live?"

"In a city called Calgary," I said. "It's in the western part of the country."

"*Si*, you have Winter Olympics last year."

"Yes," I smiled, "but I prefer summer sports. Like eating gelato in the park."

"Me too," she laughed.

In her eighties, her wit was sharp and her body was sure. Her hair was that glossy silver that all but screams high-style: shoulder-length, pulled back into a red clip. In Italian fashion, she wore a long white sweater belted at the waist with fitted blue jeans, high brown boots and brown leather gloves. Dark eyes, white teeth with red lipstick and a clear but mature complexion.

Yet her age – and her broken English – only seemed to enhance her glamor. She carried herself like a woman who was used to calling the shots. When the wind picked up, she shielded her candle to protect the flame and I caught the fragrance of her perfume.

Her first name was Camilla, but her Italian surname was either beyond my grasp or just not important enough to remember at the time.

She told me – in that worldly fractured English that made me feel like a small-town pleb in comparison – that she visited the Forum, specifically this temple, every Marzo, March, and that she had been doing so for her whole life.

I nodded, absorbing most of it. Her thick accent was as vogue as hell, but it took effort to follow.

"*Tempio di Vesta*" she said, gesturing to the white columns and circular ruins. "Me *madre*, Vestal. Me *nonna*, Vestal. Me *bisnonna*, Vestal. All women in family, Vestal. All the way back, to Gratian."

She put her hand on her chest. "I, me, is last Vestal. No *bambina*. No *figlie*, no daughters. Only sons. After me, is finish." She looked at her candle and then back at me. "You have husband? Little one?"

"No, definitely not," I said a little too quickly. "I want to go to university. Law school."

"Ah, *studente* is good. No marry man 'til *trenta, si*? Is way of Vestal." She tapped her head. "Is smart, too, *si*? Women no marry 'til thirty years old. Be much happier."

"Yes, probably," I agreed. At twenty years old, the idea of getting married and having a family was as alien as life on Mars. I gestured to her candle. "What's the candle for?"

"Goddess Vesta is sacred flame," she said with sudden gravity. "Eternal flame. Vestal priestess keep flame going in temple, all the time. Flame protect home and family. Protect wife, husband, *bambino, si*? Flame go out, *sventura*. Very bad. Vesta's flame makes things you love last forever. *La vita eterna*."

I have never been a religious person, but Camilla spoke of her faith with such affection that it was impossible to not be intrigued. I was raised in a nonreligious home and, although I had been exposed to religion through friends and extended family, it was never something that resonated with me.

Science makes sense, creationism is nonsense. Raised in a kind-hearted and good-humored family, I managed to become a decent human being without needing a supernatural savior.

Plus, I took issue with the character of an all-powerful god who did nothing to stop the suffering in the world. There was just nothing about Christianity, or the other religions that I knew of, that made me think, 'Hey, that makes sense! That gives me comfort.'

That being said, I had and have always loved religious rituals and buildings. Weddings, baptisms, even watching my friends receive Communion. I am drawn to the idea of revering something larger than myself and giving thanks for those I love, and the time I have had with them on this Earth.

Although I've never believed in a creator, I have always believed there is something sacred about my life and all life. Churches, temples, cathedrals, basilicas, monasteries, shrines, synagogues, ancient ruins of temples, you name it. I love them all.

When I was a child, there was a tiny but very pretty Orthodox Catholic church just down the road from my grandparents' house in Flin Flon, Manitoba, the zinc and copper mining town in which I was born, and which is built on the solid rock of the Canadian Shield in the northern part of the province.

My grandpa worked at the mine. So did my dad. And so did just about every other warm body in a very cold small town. Indeed, the town's name was taken from the lead character in J.E. Preston Muddock's novel *The Sunless City*.

I cannot remember how many times I rode my bicycle to the front wooden doors of this little church and tried to get in, but the doors were invariably locked.

Maybe Jesus didn't trust the locals. Or maybe, as my sometimes surly grandpa used to say, "They don't open the doors unless you have money in your hands."

My mother tells me that the church sometimes held bazaars for kids and that she took my sister and me, although I cannot recall. I only remember admiring the beautiful windows and architecture.

Living in an isolated industrial town like Flin Flon, especially in the 1970's, such a structure was positively exotic to a child's eyes. It even rivaled the sight of the Ferris wheel that miraculously went up in a parking lot in the summer of 1978, dazzling the senses out of wide-eyed kids like me as it towered up and over our heads, going round and round, its little red and blue lights blinking against the cool night sky.

Now, visiting Europe as a young adult, I was overawed by the volume, immensity and sheer spectacle of religious architecture. There wasn't a cathedral I didn't visit, and I was fortunate enough to enjoy a service in a few of them. The old wooden pews, the flying buttresses, the vaulted ceilings, the stained glass windows and the reverberating sounds of worship.

No more dropping my bike on a chipped concrete step and peering through the locked doors of a street-corner church. I gorged myself on the grandeur of Europe's holy places. And no nation worships flashier than Italy. It does churches like Las Vegas does hotels.

I told Camilla about some of the cathedrals I'd visited – Saint Peter's, Santa Maria, San Giovanni Laterno and more.

Yet she, in her fragmented English, reminded me that many of Rome's Catholic cathedrals were built from the bones of butchered temples, including the once lovely yet modest Temple of Vesta. I had spent many bright days marveling at the riches and excess of places like Vatican City, basilicas that dwarfed the throngs of star-struck human being by their soaring size and premium-priced splendor.

Now, I was sitting on a rock in the neglected ruins of a tiny temple as twilight fell, all alone save for this one truly spiritual woman burning her candle and trying, single handedly, to keep the last flickers of an ancient faith alive.

"*Ha usato essere diverso*," said Camilla. "It used to be different. This place, this *tempio*, it used to be very busy, everybody come here. Most important place."

Camilla told me that, not so long ago, millions of women, over the course of more than ten centuries, had come to this spot to honor Vesta. Only women were allowed to enter the temple, which they did with great reverence, bringing food to gift the goddess whose flame lit their homes with light and warmth, protected their family, renewed their spirit and symbolized eternal life.

In exchange, the Vestal priestesses would give them flame from Vesta's sacred fire – kept burning in the inner sanctum of the temple – to take home and burn in their own homes.

My eyes followed the tall white columns of the temple upward: despite the ruins, I could picture Vestal priestesses and Roman matrons walking among the columns, carrying the flame from Vesta's fire in candles or oil lamps, showing gratitude to the goddess and giving thanks for the blessings of life and family.

Even in the silence, I could imagine the sound of their voices in prayer, the crackling fire of Vesta lending music to their sacred lyrics.

The feral Forum cats slunk around the ancient stones at my feet like sharks swimming through a coral reef. Their self-appointed leader howled for more salami, and I dug through my pockets only to come up empty. It hissed at me. Camilla laughed and took a tin of cat treats out of her handbag, tossing them onto the grass. The cats spread out in search of them, the occasional hiss and spat interrupting her lesson.

"Vesta's fire burns with *dualita*," she said, looking into the flame of her candle. "Eternal life and rebirth."

She explained how Vesta's sacred flame burns with a dual nature: perpetuity and renewal. How it gives a woman a way to revere her existence, to celebrate and cling to those she loves, and to purify and inspire her life anew as she moves through the different eras of her own life.

She explained how it is as old and as young as Life itself, as constant and as changing. How it is a living symbol of the eternal energy in the universe, and how it manifests in our lives.

"Do you know about..." she paused, searching for the words. "*L'intuizione delle donne*...when a woman has focus, she can see more. Flame gives that focus, you understand?"

I nodded, not understanding. It was all very profound, but I was only twenty years old. I heard her words, but their meaning could only sit on the surface of my youth and inexperience like dew sits on a leaf. It would take another two decades for them to sink in.

As night fell, Camilla pulled a purple scarf out of her handbag and wrapped it around her neck. I knew it was time for me to leave. I had to walk back through the darkening Forum and I sensed that she wanted to be alone.

I held one of her hands in both of mine. "Truly, it was wonderful meeting you," I said. And I really meant it. I honestly could not remember ever having met a more fascinating person.

After sheltering her candle from a sudden chilly gust of wind, she lifted it off the stone. The flame flickered but held, and its shadow danced across one of the temple's tall, white columns. I thought again upon the hundreds of thousands of evenings that Vesta's fire burned in this spot in antiquity.

How many times had flames lit these very columns? I felt privileged to see the fire burn again, and in the presence of a Vestal, no less. I felt heartsick, too, that it no longer burned with the heat and light it once did.

"*Flamma Vesta*," said Camilla. She held the candle out to me.

I blinked at her for a moment, not understanding. Then it sunk in. "I couldn't," I said. "It means too much to you."

"*Si*, is true. You take."

Normally, I would have made a few more polite gestures of refusal before accepting; however, I knew she was sincere. She wanted me to have it and I wanted to have it. I accepted graciously and then I left her alone at her temple, to commune with her goddess and the generations of Vestal priestesses before her. I stumbled out of the Forum, letting the candle burn until the wind had its way.

And I kept stumbling for a while. Out of Italy, back to Canada, through university. My surreal experience with Camilla at the Temple of Vesta sparked an interest in the Classics and, for the next four years of my pre-law undergraduate degree, I studied Latin, Art History, Ancient History, Greco-Roman History, Roman Religion and Mythology. If it had the words "Rome" or "history" or "ancient" anywhere in the course description, I signed up.

Although Camilla had made a great impact on me, it wasn't until these undergrad years that I was able to fill in the blanks of her words with real knowledge. The language barrier had left me wondering about many of the things she had said, or had tried to say.

More than once, I would be sitting in the middle of a packed lecture hall when the professor would reference the Vestal order or its banishment. I would have to fight the urge to jump from my seat and shout, "So that's what she was talking about!"

The more I learned about the history of the Vesta tradition, the more I realized that Camilla had used our time together to tell me as much about its spiritual aspect as she could. I could get facts from textbooks, but what Camilla had to teach could only have come from her.

Yet the textbooks had a lot to teach, too. I learned that the Vestals who kept the sacred fire burning were held in the highest of esteem and were Rome's only state-funded priesthood. It was believed that the eternal Flame of Vesta represented Rome itself, and that as long as it burned, the Roman Empire and way of life would endure.

It was only when the new Christian emperors forcibly extinguished Vesta's fire in the 4th century CE and criminalized her worship – all amid intense public outcry and despair – that the great empire collapsed.

That put a piece of the puzzle in place. Camilla had said that the women in her family had been Vestals, "All the way back, to Gratian." The Emperor Gratian was the first to banish the Vestal tradition and close the temple. After he came to power, Camilla's Vestal ancestors would have had no choice but to keep the sacred flame burning in secret. Had they been discovered, the flame would have been extinguished and they would have been executed.

I thought back to Camilla and her high Italian leather boots, her red lipstick and palpable confidence. The old girl had even more game in her than I had realized.

After my undergraduate degree, I trudged through law school and then began working. My obsession with history became part of my history. There was no more looking to the past. Now, I was looking to the future law career that I was expected to shine in. My life became a blur of legal statutes, common law cases, precedents, appeals, client files and court dates.

I met my husband at thirty years old and married a year later. It was never a conscious decision to adopt the Vestal way that Camilla had advised but, with my single-minded focus on education and career, it did work out that way. Or perhaps Camilla had planted a seed.

Regardless, it was all working out as planned. I was on the fast-track to the child-free lifestyle and high-powered, self-important law career of my dreams. And with each passing year, the dreams became more grandiose and egocentric. If you've ever had lunch with a law student or a lawyer, you know exactly what I'm talking about.

And the Flamma Vesta? I forgot about it. Camilla? She became one of a thousand passersby as my life sped on. Her candle – the one that burned with the sacred Flame of Vesta – lay stuffed unceremoniously in a ratty backpack in my mom's basement, buried under boxes of old clothes and trinkets for decades, just as the Temple of Vesta had lain buried under the rubble of the Roman Forum for so many centuries, its hearth smashed and its flame snuffed out.

Camilla may have been looking for a worthy successor to carry on her ancient tradition; however, what she found was an utterly self-focused girl who was all too easily consumed by her own single-minded drive and never-happy disposition. It would take over twenty years for that girl to grow up and realize what she wanted from life. And what life wanted from her.

It is that realization – more of a slipshod sort of enlightenment, really – that this book is about.

As you'll see, it took a near-death experience, a failed career, a stalled marriage and finally a good bitch-slap from Camilla from beyond the grave to get me there, but then again, I was never a fast learner. Or maybe light just shines brightest in the darkest of places.

Perhaps you've been in that dark place, too. there now. There is an unhappiness epidemic, a spiri sweeping through the lives of too many women. The disappointed, regretful and sad, and sometimes have n They feel empty and uncertain. Divorce and family bre regularly rip apart lives and leave in their wake a trail oi bitter women and heartbroken kids.

Women are left feeling lost, afraid and alone in the world as they struggle to cope with loss – loss of youth, opportunity, relationships, dreams, energy and hope – and to deal with the many ups-and-downs of life. For too many women, the flame of faith and happiness no longer burns in their lives.

But I've learned – the hard way, of course – that it is possible to reignite and renew that flame. If that can happen, more women will find joy, meaning and sacredness within the walls of their own home. More women will celebrate their lives. More relationships will endure. More children will learn that family is forever. More women will feel grounded and at peace with the universe and their place in it, even as life continues to twist and turn, to give and take.

Like the mythical phoenix, Vesta must therefore rise from the ashes and once again use her eternal flame – indeed, it has never completely gone out – to light a path for women to revere and renew their lives in a relevant, radiant and uniquely feminine way. It's time for her to share her Old World secret with the New World.

CHAPTER I

Playing with Fire

Experience is the teacher of all things.
  - Gaius Julius Caesar, 100 BCE – 44 BCE

Humanius est deridere vitam quam deplorare. (It is better to laugh at life than to lament over it).
  - Heraclitus, Greek Philosopher, 535 – 475 BCE

    I got married the year that I finished law school. I have no idea what compelled me to cram two major life events into so close a space – maybe I'm stress junkie – but I did. Everyone told me not to do it. My mom, my sister, my friends. They all said, "You can't write law school finals and plan a wedding. It's a bad idea to start a marriage and a career at the same time…it's just too much at once. "
    I remember my best friend wagging her finger at me and saying, "You're playing with fire and you're gonna get burned. Slow down. Why are you always in such a rush? Why are you never happy with where you are?"

The Master Plan

At that time, my life was a master plan and there no way I was going to change it on account of something as banal as good advice. This master plan included a checklist with two columns. "Get It" and "Avoid It Like The Plague."

In the Get It column, were a prestigious law career, my own corner office with a window, a fantastic wardrobe full of pencil skirts and designer handbags, Italian tiles for my house and a Porsche 911 Turbo for my driveway, season tickets to the opera, a cottage on Salt Spring Island, and a body that never, ever gave birth to anything that would cry, crap, spit up or ruin my life.

In the Avoid It Like The Plague column were a breadmaking machine (tied with a slow cooker and a sewing machine), jeans with an elastic waist, women's daytime talk shows, wearing a bathrobe all day, driving a minivan, shopping at bulk food stores, knowing how to make more than two kinds of casserole, living in suburbia or giving birth to anything that would cry, crap, spit up or ruin my life.

All was going according to plan, too. My new husband Don was as sexy as he was supportive, and he displayed a suitable amount of awe at my academic accomplishments and fledgling law career. He had a "manly" job in the oil and gas industry that I felt was the perfect accessory to my brainer, more urbane career choice. My waistline had never been smaller and my future had never been bigger. And why not? I was living by my Get It checklist. I was sticking to my own master plan. What could go wrong?

I remember the day several years earlier that my sister told me she was pregnant. We were both in university. It was just before supper (and final exams) that she showed up unannounced at my apartment door, wearing a green winter jacket and sporting that regrettable "Rachel" haircut that all the girls got when the sitcom *Friends* was popular. I opened the door and she stood in the doorway, bawling her eyes out.

"What's wrong?" I asked, holding up a spaghetti spoon as it dripped sauce onto the floor.

She cried harder.

"Did your cat die?" I asked. "Did the TV fall on him?"

Now, if that seems like a stupidly random thing to ask, I must say that I had my reasons. The TV had actually fallen on the cat the day before, but he had escaped unscathed. Maybe *Friends* was on and the poor creature was trying to change channels.

She looked into my eyes. She *glared* into my eyes. "I'm pregnant! My life is over!"

As she stumbled into my apartment, throwing her backpack against the wall and collapsing face-down onto the couch, I closed the door behind her. "No, of course your life isn't over!" I said.

But you know what? I totally thought that her life was over.

Conception and Denial

The distant memory of my sister's melodramatic pregnancy announcement was the last thing on my mind that cold February morning when I found myself lying bloated on my couch, a row of various antacids on my coffee table.

I had been feeling a little run down and achy in the abdomen, but assumed it was just some work stress. I called in sick and watched a few minutes of *The View*; however, that only made me feel worse, so I reached for the remote control to turn off the television.

That's when it flashed across the screen: a commercial for a home pregnancy test.

I sat up straight. When was my period due?

In fifteen minutes, I was back from the drug store and peeing on a stick. Forget the years of training it took to plead a case in front of a judge. My entire being was now focused on pleading for mercy in front of a pregnancy test stick.

But that "+" sign is a ruthless little control freak. I stumbled from the bathroom to the living room and collapsed face-down onto the couch. "My life is over!"

Have you ever heard of the Kubler-Ross model? It is a psychology hypothesis that talks about the five emotional stages that a person goes through when she is facing an unwanted or terrible fate: denial, anger, depression, bargaining and acceptance. Without lifting myself off the couch, I raced through these five stages at break-neck speed, and then back-tracked to denial where I pretty much set up shop.

I looked at my dog. He was sitting beside the couch with his head cocked quizzically.

"My life won't change a bit," I told him. "I'll bring the baby to my office with me. Babies sleep a lot, right? It can just go under my desk while I'm working...maybe in a designer bassinet so it looks good. My clients won't even know it's there. If I have court, I'll just feed it lots so that it sleeps through the whole thing. No need to change plans. No need to panic."

He pretended to see something interesting on the floor and sniffed at it. I had taken delusional thinking to a whole new level. Even the dog could see it.

Crash and Burn

At the beginning of my third trimester, I visited my OB/GYN for a regular prenatal checkup. Since her office was in Edmonton, Alberta, an hour's drive from where I lived, my mom came with me so we could hit West Edmonton Mall afterward. That, and have a piece of chocolate cheesecake at our favorite restaurant. What's the point of being pregnant if you can't eat for two.

You know those blissful expecting women who stay in amazing shape, eat only organic food and do yoga while they're pregnant? That wasn't me. I took care of myself and my unborn baby, but pregnancy was not a state I relished. More than once I looked at my belly with the same suspicion that Sigourney Weaver looked at hers in the *Aliens* movie.

I sat impatiently in the exam room while an intern came in and introduced herself. After some small talk, she asked me to roll up my sleeve and she wrapped the blood pressure cuff around my arm, pumping it up until it was snug.

As the pressure released, her eyes darted from the clock on the wall to me. Very quickly – too quickly – she unwrapped the cuff and stepped out of the room saying, "I'll be right back."

And she was right back. Within moments she returned with my OB/GYN in tow. The intern stood back with a wrinkled brow while my doctor re-took my blood pressure. As the pressure in the cuff released, she looked at me. "You're going to blow a gasket, woman," she said. "Your blood pressure's through the roof." She took it again, and then turned to her intern. "Get her checked into the hospital."

"What?" I said. "I'm supposed to go shopping right now." That sounded ridiculous, so I tried again. "I have clients. I have court tomorrow."

"Well, you have pre-eclampsia today," she said, "and you'll be staying in the hospital until the baby comes."

"For two months? I can't stay in the hospital for two months!"

"You can and you will," she said flatly. "Your blood pressure has to come down, or neither of you are going to make it. Clear your calendar."

Within an hour, my skyrocketing blood pressure and I were wearing an open-backed hospital gown and sitting, cross-legged and shell-shocked, on a hospital bed as an assembly line of neonatology specialists visited my room.

They gave me injections to speed up the baby's lung development in case he was born early, but I knew that wouldn't happen. I knew the pregnancy would go to full-term. Doctors think they know it all.

As it turned out, they did know it all. Only three days later, at two o'clock in the morning, the baby became "distressed" and was delivered by emergency Caesarean section.

I was barely into my seventh month of pregnancy and he weighed only two pounds. I remember seeing him for the first time, curled up in the middle of an incubator, as I blinked to clear the post-anesthetic fog from my eyes. A translucent, skinny red frog with a ventilator down his throat and a doll-sized blue wool cap on his head.

Forget the Get It list, forget the years of school and studies, forget the office, forget the career and the pencil skirts. I dropped out of my life and planted myself beside his incubator in the Neonatal Intensive Care Unit, becoming an expert on every bing and bleep of his medical monitor.

The kid was Hercules. Within a week, the medical staff labelled him a "grower and feeder." That's a preemie who has no serious medical issues, and who only needs to finish in the incubator what he should have finished in my incompetent tyrant of a uterus. Don and I took him home two months later, when he was five pounds, a virtual giant in the world of the NICU.

'Okay,' I thought,' we got through that. 'Now back to the plan.' The original baby plan was for me to stay home for six months, go back to work part-time for another six months and then return to full-time work when the baby was one year old.

For a woman working in a law firm, even that was a career-threatening length of time to be out of the game. I tried not to think about all the uterus-free men that were vying for my job during my absence.

There was just one slight problem: pneumonia. A premature baby is very susceptible to respiratory illness, meaning that even the common cold could land him back in the hospital, back on a ventilator, back fighting for his life.

After a few months, I began to check out daycares in the city, but each time I was greeted by a throng of toddlers with runny noses, dirty hands and stained shirts. To a germaphobe like me, a daycare is basically a cheerily painted hell.

I recall walking up to the doors of one daycare center – probably the nicest and most expensive facility in the city – and seeing a sign taped to the window. It said, "Please Be Advised That We Are Experiencing An Outbreak Of Hand, Foot And Mouth Disease."

I turned around and went back to my car. I could feel the building blocks of my life, my master plan, crashing down around me. I sat back in the driver's seat and stared out the windshield where I suddenly saw words, the most dreaded words I could imagine, scrolling non-stop across the glass.

Housewife. Stay-At-Home Mom. Women's Daytime Talk Shows. Elastic Waists. Bathrobe. Bulk Food Stores. Casseroles. Housewife. Stay-At-Home Mom . . . .

In the end, none of us can escape our destiny. We are all playthings of the Fates, those three sisters who spin, measure and cut the threads of our lives as they wish. These mystical ladies weaved for me a life that I had spent my adulthood reviling and avoiding. The life of a mother. Worse, a stay-at-home mother. A housewife. What could be more boring or unfulfilling? The wings on my feet were clipped and I was sidelined from the action. I emotionally relocated from denial to acceptance.

Strangely enough, at a time when Vesta should have been most relevant to me – housebound and smack in the middle of family life – she was pushed out of my thoughts. I was too preoccupied with trying to keep my son healthy and cold-free for his first winter.

That's a full-time job when you live in Canada, the breeding ground of every cold and flu strain known to humankind. I put away the law books and broke out the bleach. My life centered around disinfecting, hand-washing and, for a dismayed while, women's daytime talk shows.

Acceptance

But something weird was happening to me. This stay-at-home mom gig wasn't so bad after all. Who knew, but our son turned out to be the cutest, smartest, funniest, most fascinating little creature that ever crawled on all-fours or spontaneously fell asleep in the middle of the kitchen floor while gnawing on an ice-cream sandwich.

I used to think, 'There's no way I'm going to change diapers.' Now, I thought, 'There's no way anybody else is going to change his diapers.'

I became one of those moms who called their friends when the baby threw his sippy cup against the wall in that oh-so adorable way, and who leaned over the railing of his crib when he was sleeping, just to listen to those sweet little breaths and watch that sleeper-clad tummy go up and down. Sickening stuff.

I didn't watch the world like I used to. Now I watched him as he watched the world. I didn't watch the fireworks, I watched him watching the fireworks. I didn't laugh when the cat did something funny, I laughed at him laughing at the cat. I didn't enjoy the warmth of the bathwater, I enjoyed him enjoying the warmth of the bathwater. I had tunnel vision, tunnel love, tunnel attention, just for him.

So when the official "You're Fired" letter came from my office, the shock of my total career failure was mercifully absorbed by the almost dangerous levels of maternal hormones that had supersaturated my brain and body.

I shrugged my shoulders, nibbled on a teething biscuit and scribbled a grocery list on the back of the envelope. 'Hmm,' I thought, 'what kind of casserole should I make for supper tonight?'

I sat back on the couch and brushed bits of teething biscuit off my bathrobe. It was early afternoon, and I was still wearing it.

I squeezed the belly of a stuffed Teletubby until it made some indecipherable statement followed by the trademark Teletubby *Eh-Oh!* and my son collapsed onto the floor in a fit of whole-body laughter. Then he fell asleep at my slippered feet, spent from the sheer hilarity of it all.

I channel-surfed until I landed on the flagship of women's daytime talk shows, the *Oprah Winfrey Show*. Wow, did the kids at law school despise her. You weren't cool if you watched Oprah. You weren't a critical thinker. You were one of the unwashed masses. You were a drone.

Whatever. *The Young and the Restless* didn't start for another couple of hours and my son was nap-twitching beside me on the couch. What else was I going to do? Exercise or something crazy like that?

I remember that particular episode with terror-charged clarity. According to the show, a study revealed that one in three married men cheat. Why? Boredom. Familiarity. Feeling unappreciated. A child-centered marriage. Lack of sex. 'I never saw it coming,' said a broken-hearted wife.

I put down the box of teething biscuits and took a quick inventory.

Breadmaking machine? Check. Shopping at bulk food stores? Check. Knowing how to make more than two kinds of casserole? Check. Living in suburbia? Check. Giving birth? Check. Women's daytime talk shows? Check. Jeans with an elastic waist? No – most days I didn't put on pants. Wearing a bathrobe all day? I looked down at my worn terrycloth robe, and then it hit me. I was one mini-van away from a cheating husband.

The good news is that I had settled comfortably into stage five of the Kubler-Ross model, that being acceptance. The bad news is that I had created my own version of stage six: complacency.

CHAPTER II

From the Ashes

Much of your pain is self-chosen. It is the bitter potion by which the physician within you heals your sick self.
  - Kahlil Gibran, *The Prophet*. Lebanese Poet, 1883 – 1931 CE

There is a certain pleasure in weeping.
  - Ovid, Roman Poet, 43 BCE – 17 CE

After the bathrobe awakening, I knew I needed a kick in my complacency. I started to think about returning to work; however, I had given up on my dream of being the world's greatest lawyer. It just wasn't that important to me anymore. Plus, there was no way I could put in the billable hours required and still be the kind of mom that I wanted to be. It was part-time or nothing.

This all happened at a fairly convenient time. My parents were scaling back their transportation company, so my mom had more time to watch my son which she was always eager to do.

Don had received a work promotion that came with an office job and a liberal schedule, so he was around more as well. He was a very hands-on, happy dad. I had the kind of backup that most moms can only dream about.

Scared Straight

So I decided to start my own part-time divorce mediation practice. Believe it or not, it was the best thing that ever happened to my marriage. Why? Because my job gave me a birds-eye view of what a failed marriage looked like.

I was living a career version of *Scared Straight!* that 1970's documentary about a group of young offenders who are given an up close and personal tour of a prison where hardened lifers yell, swear and threaten them. The goal was to motivate the kids, through fear, to stay out of jail and to walk the straight and narrow instead. The fear tactic worked for them, and it worked for me, too.

I saw how my clients had run their relationships into the ground. How they talked to each other with contempt, criticism and self-centeredness. How they stopped showing each other affection, appreciation and adoration. How they let themselves go, let sex slip off the radar, let their kids call the shots, let it all slip away.

And how they were now sitting in my office, pretending to be interested in the art on the walls, while really they were scared out of their wits that they were going to lose custody of their kids, ownership of their home, half the assets they had spent years toiling for, the respect of family and friends and a lifestyle they used to love.

I started to think about how I had treated Don for the few years of our marriage. Since bringing our son home from the hospital, I had turned into something of a tyrant. I expected him to be at my beck and call, like I was some kind of royalty and he was my personal servant. Control, contempt, criticism – I did them all in my own subtle way. Not all the time, but enough.

And our life definitely revolved around our child. The baby's cradle was still beside our bed and Don often joked that our son would still be sleeping in our bedroom when he was in junior high. It was a jibe I ignored, even though I knew it was his way of gently asking when we could have our privacy as husband and wife back. Looking back, I hate to think what was going through his head.

So I started to clean up my act. I caught myself when I heard a nasty tone in my voice, and I replaced it with a friendlier one. I made it a habit to show or speak appreciation at least once a day. I asked him more about his hobbies and pretended to be fascinated as he went on and on and on about air-cooled Volkswagens. I openly praised him in front of our family and friends.

Through sheer force of will, I let him parent our son the way he wanted to, and stopped giving him "advice" about how to do it right. That was excruciating. Didn't he know that our son liked a glass of warm milk *after* his pajamas were on, and not before? Sheesh. I started to trust his judgment as a husband and father. I hit the lingerie shops, put our son to bed on a regular schedule so that we had time and energy for sex, and began to initiate more often. Soon, our marriage had never been better.

But then something really weird started to happen. Things were so good at home that I started to bring some of that positive energy to work with me. I found that it affected the way I interacted with my clients and, more importantly, the way they interacted with each other. My mediation sessions went from serious and stressful to pleasant and even humorous at times.

Some of my separated clients – husbands and wives who had been estranged – started to say that they hadn't had such an enjoyable or insightful conversation with each other in years. Of course I had wanted my clients to connect. I just hadn't expected them to re-connect. More and more, couples came to see me to see whether their marriages could be saved.

They said that I was their last-stop before divorce court. I'd laugh it off and say, "Oh, thanks, no pressure." But to be honest I didn't feel too much pressure. They had already decided to divorce, so they and I didn't have much to lose at that point. If they could work it out, it was a bonus all around.

The Rebound

I did my best to help this new wave of clients see whether their marriages could rebound from whatever problems were plaguing them. I taught them better communication skills, how to manage intense emotion, how to challenge their assumptions, be more empathetic, improve the way they interacted on a day to day basis, and get on the same page in terms of parenting, priorities, expectations and money. I taught them how to resolve specific conflicts, from in-law battles to broken trust, as well as strategies to make positive changes last.

I also started authoring relationship and intimacy guides that encouraged couples to have more fun in bed and connect on an emotional and physical level. Most of the sex guides out there at the time were either too disgusting or too diluted, so with Don's bemused help I wrote mainstream books geared toward long-term, committed couples who wanted to kick it up a gear in the bedroom without getting grossed out in the process.

My approach was a good one. It was popular too, and my practice thrived until I was one of the busiest and most referred practitioners in my region. After the books garnered some strong reviews from the media, I became a relationship expert in Canada and the United States, regularly appearing in newspapers and glossy magazines, and doing guest spots on television and radio. It seemed like I had all the answers.

So I made it official: I stopped doing divorce mediation altogether, and focused exclusively on couples' reconciliatory mediation. Believe it or not, it was the worst thing that ever happened to my marriage.

Taking My Work Home With Me

In theory, the idea of focusing on reconciliation rather than divorce would make things easier on me. In practice, the shift made my job a lot harder.

Many people who are going through the divorce process have a let's-just-get-this-over-with attitude. They're done. They've screamed, yelled, cried to the point of exhaustion and apathy, and they just don't give a shit anymore. That can make them fairly accommodating. "Whatever, I just want this to be over."

The big decision – to end the marriage – has already been made. Now it's only a matter of hammering out the details: distribution of assets, child custody and access, child support payments, taxes and so on. It's all about logistics.

Not so with couples who are still trying to save their relationship. For these folks, the rage, betrayal, sorrow and uncertainty are at their peak. These people are often more difficult to handle because, in addition to the specific and sometimes very nasty relationship problems that need to be resolved, there is this overwhelming fear of the unknown.

Will it work out? Is he or she just going to screw around on me again? Can we ever get back what we had? Am I just wasting my life with this selfish, condescending, short-tempered son of a bitch?

Worse, these people are often eager to share the gory details of their partner's transgressions, real or imagined. That was something that hadn't happened all that much when I mediated divorces. Now, it was all I heard. And it was sometimes a struggle to avoid getting sucked into the ugly quicksand of their emotion and drama.

Imagine spending the bulk of your day, day after day, listening to a woman fume about how selfish, immature, untrustworthy, unfaithful, irritating, self-indulgent, angry, critical and narcissistic her husband has become, and how awful and empty and wasted her life has turned out to be.

Imagine listening to her talk about how his affair "came out of nowhere" or how he had "used her up." How he "took everything she had" and "turned their children against her." How she was unhappy, unfulfilled and depressed because, in the end, men always screw up and disappoint and lives always fall apart. Any woman who doesn't think so is just fooling herself. Just wait, my dear, the axe will fall in your marriage, too. It's just a matter of time.

Imagine listening to her lament her lost youth, weight gain, sagging breasts, missed opportunities and shattered faith. How each day is more pointless than the last. How she is lonely and life hasn't turned out the way she wanted it to. How she wished she could just start all over again. How she wished, some days, that her husband would get hit by a truck so that she could collect his life insurance policy and then dance on his grave with the revenge boy toy she just met through an online dating site.

When you're sitting in a room with a woman who is at the lowest point in her life, she says a lot of despondent, hopeless things. Things that you don't usually hear people say around the water cooler at work. Even though I am a mediator and not a counselor, people still unload. And that kind of negative energy has a way of moving across a room and landing right on top of you.

I held steady for a few years, but eventually I started to bring my work home with me. That's always a bad thing, but when your job is marriage mediation, it's a *really* bad thing.

If a client complained that her husband ignored her and spent all his time texting his buddies, I'd get irritated the moment Don checked his text messages during dinner, even if he was on-call at work. I'd let out an exasperated sigh and leave the table.

If a client complained that her husband spent all his time watching Internet porn, I'd look at Don with suspicion every time he went downstairs to look up movie show times on the computer. Maybe movie times wasn't the only thing he was looking up.

'Come to think of it, he hasn't been initiating sex as much as he used to,' I'd say to myself. 'Never mind that he's stressed at work and I've been a complete wench, he should still be working up a sweat trying to romance me.'

If a client complained that her husband never did anything with the kids, I'd watch Don's every move around the house. How many times did he talk to our son? For how long did he play with him? Did he read him a bedtime story and tuck him in, or did he leave it for me to do? If our son donned a superhero cape or held up a Lego creation to show him and he didn't *instantly* break into wild applause, I'd bitch that he wasn't paying enough attention to his child.

If a client complained that her husband never helped around the house, I started to notice how often I emptied the dishwasher versus how often Don did it. If she said that her husband had stopped doing the little things, I would wonder why Don hadn't brought me flowers in months. He was starting to take me for granted. What an asshole. I started to assume that every move he made, every word he spoke, had a hidden, sinister motive.

People are often angry during mediation. Some of my female clients were quite snarky, while some of my male clients were belligerent. Some men tried to control the mediation session with the same tactics I assumed they used at home to get their way: loud voices, profanity and body language that emphasized their bulk or strength. Like a peacock spreading its feathers.

Of course, their behavior didn't have the same effect in my office. I had been trained to deal with high-conflict people and situations, and could quickly flip the switch from friendly to allow-me-to-put-you-in-your-place.

If you've ever seen a TV lawyer ask the judge permission to treat a difficult or uncooperative witness as a "hostile witness," you've seen the switch. And on those rare occasions that I couldn't establish control, I simply ended the session and let them know I wasn't getting paid enough to put up with their childish bullshit.

The side-effect of this, however, was that I started to walk around with a chip on my shoulder. I was used to being the boss. I was used to calling the shots. As a fairly small woman, I definitely had a touch of the female Napoleon complex. And unfortunately, I started to bring that part of my work home with me, too.

If I didn't get my way, whether it was over what we were having for supper or how we'd spend our money, I'd speak to Don as though he were an unreasonable client and I'd shut him down on the spot. I'd use my gazillion years of language and legal training to talk circles around him, put him in his place, and treat every disagreement like a criminal trial I had to win.

My clients were getting the best of me, and my husband was getting the worst.

From Anger to Apathy

But not all of my clients came in with angry expressions or sat down with their arms crossed and their eyes full of contempt for each other. Some came in wearing pleasant smiles, even holding hands. They sat down politely and quietly, waiting and hoping that I could work a miracle for them. These were my toughest clients.

It was the wife who said, "He's such a wonderful man. I could never ask for better father for my kids. He works so hard. He is so kind. I don't know why I'm not happy," and her husband who replied, "I love her so much. I just want her to be happy. I don't know why she isn't happy. I'll do anything to make her happy."

It was the woman who felt like life was ultimately meaningless and that she was wasting her existence washing dishes and driving the kids to hockey practice and having routine sex with a husband she loved but couldn't bear to be around for more than five minutes because his very presence reminded her how bored she was.

It was the woman who felt that life was, in a word, blah. And who was beginning to think that her marriage and home life were standing in the way of happiness.

She didn't *blame* them. She just wondered whether she'd be happier without them. This is the kind of woman who hasn't yet bailed from her marriage or home life, but who feels adrift in her own life. She has a great husband and family, nice house, good job, money in the bank.

What do you say to the woman who has it all, who knows she has it all, and yet is still unhappy? Who still feels apathetic about her own life? Sometimes I would encourage her to challenge her expectations. That's always a handy fallback when nothing else seems to work.

Other times, I would refer her away to a therapist or pastor, only to have her call me back a few months down the road to tell me that nothing worked and to ask whether she could come back again to talk to me; however, I didn't want to see her again. I didn't know what to tell her.

Plus, her emotions were contagious. When I couldn't answer her questions or give her advice, I was left asking the same questions and needing the same advice. Her search for meaning, fulfillment and happiness was rubbing off on me, and unfortunately I started taking that part of my work home with me, too.

Cold and Miserable

Although I had always enjoyed the usual movie-and-popcorn-then-sex Friday nights with Don, I started to see them differently. They were mundane and predictable. Wasn't there more to life? Was I wasting my life watching movies with my husband instead of climbing a mountain somewhere and finding my own personal guru in Bali?

On those cold Canadian winter nights when we'd sit in front of the fireplace reading and sipping hot chocolate, listening to our son play video games or laugh out loud at some comic he was reading, I'd stare at the dark sky and piles of snow outside and imagine my toes sinking into the warm sands at Elafonissi as the hot Mediterranean sun beat down on my face.

Life was passing me by. It was dead and frozen outside. No birds chirping, no leaves on the trees, no flowers on the ground, no kids jumping on the trampoline in the backyard.

I'd sigh heavily and tell Don that I hated the cold. I hated winter. I hated the eight months of living in a deep freeze while the rest of the world's population was being warmed by the sun, was free to walk outside without eight layers of clothes and had the simple pleasure of looking up at the starry sky without their face getting frostbitten. I hated my life. Because I was cold.

Poor guy. He didn't know what to say or what to do, so he said and did everything he could. He told me how much loved me and how great our life was. We had each other, a fantastic kid, great house and well-paying jobs that gave us far more freedom than most. We lived in a quaint little historic town with friendly people, low crime and top-notch schools. All winter long, he'd try to keep my spirits up with his non-stop sense of humor and even temperament.

He bought me rhino-sized flowering cactus gardens, put sky-blue light panels in the ceiling and installed artificial sun lamps in my office. He renovated the bathroom and set it up so that I could take hot milk baths in luxury while watching my favorite soap opera on a wall-mounted television. He always pre-warmed the heating blanket before I crawled into bed.

He booked mid-winter vacations to Louisiana for hot and sweaty swamp tours, California to walk along sunny Zuma Beach, and then to the Mojave Desert where we'd drive into the middle of nowhere at night and stargaze into the black desert sky. We'd go anyplace that the mercury rose above 80° Fahrenheit. We'd have a wonderful time.

But then our plane would touch down back home in Calgary and we'd have to open our luggage to put our winter boots back on. We'd walk outside the terminal and the minus 40° Fahrenheit temperature would freeze my face and the snow would spill over the top of my boots before the shuttle bus even arrived to take us back to our frozen car.

I'd sit shivering in the car on the drive back to our house, pouting like a spoiled brat, while Don tried to cheer me up by talking about how nice it would be to sleep in our own bed and how we'd take an even longer vacation next winter. At the rate we were vacationing in sunny places, we'd never be able to retire to one.

It must have been exhausting for him. No matter what he tried, he couldn't make me happy. Although I loved him deeply, I felt myself pulling away. I started to see a certain look in his eyes. "I don't know why you're unhappy, I don't know how to make you happy, and it's scaring the hell out of me."

It was the same look I'd seen in my office from throngs of worried, confused men who didn't know why their unhappy wife had one foot out the door, or what they could do to make her come back inside.

This rampant unhappiness wasn't limited to my married clients, either. Very few women around me were truly happy. Whether they were single, divorced or dating, whether they had kids or cats, they felt burdened by memories or mistakes they had made, or simply felt weighed down by life and its questions and disappointments. Family estrangements had left many feeling abandoned and alone in the world.

It seemed like everyone was looking for a fresh start, a well-lit path, that they just couldn't find. Everybody was so lost.

Some jumped from bed to bed. Others struck up fake friendships on social networking sites, started popping pills, hit the bottle or maxed out their credit cards on make-over wardrobes and soul-searching vacations. Some retreated back to the church they were raised in, only to find its doctrines as irrelevant or alienating as ever. Others grew bitter and apathetic and just gave up.

I asked myself whether my expectations were too high. Was I just impossible to please? Did I just need some perspective and a dose of reality? I'd call my sister – an operating room nurse – and she'd tell me that both she and I needed to "count our blessings" because of some tragic case she saw that day.

She'd tell me about the parents who just took their child off life support. Or the woman who hemorrhaged and bled to death after giving birth to her child. Or the sixty-year-old wife who stood by the bedside of her husband, who had just died on the operating table, and spent an hour wiping the blood and sputum off his face and thanking him for the life they had together.

I'd wholeheartedly agree with her. "Yes, we have it so good. We are so lucky. We need to count our blessings." I believed it. But the feeling of gratitude and fulfillment only lasted an hour, and then I would be back to questioning the meaning of it all, cursing the cold and feeling miserable about my own life.

CHAPTER III

Las Vesta

The wheel is come full circle.
- Shakespeare, *King Lear.* English Playwright, 1564 – 1616 CE

The unexamined life is not worth living.
- Socrates, Greek Philosopher, 470 – 399 BCE

Around this time – November of 2012 – Don and I flew down to Las Vegas for a wedding. The last thing I wanted to do was attend a wedding. It's hard to witness that much happiness when you're running low on it yourself.

Plus, I was overwhelmed at work. Impatient clients, writing deadlines, media gigs that took too much preparation and ate up too much time. Our son was just recovering from a nasty flu and the house was a disaster.

I made excuse after excuse, but Don was insistent that we go. We needed it, he said. We'd been getting on each other's nerves, and we needed the time away. So off we went.

On the day of the wedding, we spent the morning sipping fancy coffees and wandering around Caesar's Palace. I always get a kick out of touring the reproductions of Roman sculptures, architecture and art. Yet despite the surroundings and the freedom of being away from home, we had barely said ten words to each other all morning.

At one point, Don tried to hold my hand – a gesture of peace – but I quickly took it away and pretended to check for text messages on my phone. A few minutes later, he suggested that we head to a gift shop to buy a souvenir for our son. I'd normally be all over that. But again, I shrugged indifferently and just kept walking.

Eventually, we stumbled into a classically-themed outdoor wedding chapel. And as we strolled over the smooth stone of the pathway, past the gurgling fountains, greenery and Roman statues, I saw something that made me stop in my tracks.

A Blast From the Past

Directly in front of me was the Temple of Vesta. I blinked. Of course, it was smaller and plainer than the real temple in Rome, but it was white and round with marble columns encircling the tiny inner sanctum. With only the slightest bit of imagination, one could feel the heat of a burning fire within, and imagine the white-robed figures of Vestal priestesses walking past the pillars.

In an instant, it all came back. Images and emotions and thoughts swirled through my head. I was twenty years old, tossing bits of a stale salami sandwich to stray cats and holding my coat closed against a chilly Italian breeze.

I was on the Via Sacra as twilight fell, with the ruins of the Roman Forum all around me. I had no husband, I had no child, and I was unrecognizable to my present self. I had never been to university and I had no career. I did, however, have wings on my feet.

I could hear Camilla's voice, smell her perfume, even see the lines around her eyes as she smiled and wrapped her purple scarf around her neck.

I could see her shelter her candle from the wind and then hold it up against the darkening sky as I watched the shadows of its flames dance along the cracks of the ancient columns. I could see the feral Forum cats slinking around the ancient stones and moving through the tall grass, howling for scraps. I was there a second time, no different than the first.

My throat tightened as I struggled not to cry, although I'm not sure what was causing the tears. The memory of someone or someplace I knew in my youth? The freedom? How different my life was – husband, child, housework, demanding career – than I had expected it to be?

And then it hit me. They were tears of happiness. In all our years of marriage, Don had never said an unkind word to me. He made me laugh every day. He was the most fun, interesting, smartest, sexiest and decent man I'd ever known and he treated me like a queen. If I was blue, he'd bring me a glass of my favorite red wine.

If I was sick, he'd run out at midnight to get medicine. If I was happy, he'd celebrate with me. He was the other half of the coolest kid that ever was, and he was a fantastic father to him. Our son was happy, healthy, creative and intelligent, and he was growing up with all his dad's best qualities.

For the second time in my life, I heard Camilla speaking. "Flame protect home and family. Protect wife, husband, *bambino, si?*" I remembered her lesson: how her faith encouraged a woman to celebrate and cling to what she loved, and how it could inspire her life anew as she moved, with grace and gratitude, through the changing phases and challenges of her life.

I was exactly where she knew I would be – at the crossroads of a changing life and needing direction. Needing faith.

As a twenty-year-old, unmarried and child-free atheist, her words – and her faith – had been lost on me. I had always felt deeply privileged to have met her and cherished our time together. I knew she was far wiser than I was; however, I just didn't have the life experience at that time to truly appreciate what she was telling me.

Now, in my forties, it all made sense. The dew was sinking into the leaf. She had given me the flame of faith and, even though I hadn't bothered to re-light it, it had nonetheless been illuminating my way to this very spot, this very time.

I think that was the first time in my impatient, never-enough life that I had truly, in the deepest part of me, felt reverence for my life, my husband and my son. It was like stepping into the clarity of pure sunshine after making a long, convoluted passage in the dark, a passage that began among the bare ruins of Rome and ended, of all places, in the opulence of Las Vegas.

Don took my hand and we sat on a stone bench.

"Why are you crying?" he said. His voice was hoarse. Who knows, maybe he thought I was going to say something awful. "Do you want to go home?"

"No," I said. "Let's just sit here for a few minutes."

"We can sit here as long as you like."

I laughed. "Stop being nice. It just makes me feel worse." I squeezed his hand and, for the first time in a long time, saw him actually smile. A real smile.

Basement Excavations

When we arrived back home, I went straight to my mom's house. I dug through boxes and boxes of books, trinkets, keepsakes and unpardonable 80's shoulder-padded shirts in her basement until I found what I was looking for.

It was wrapped unceremoniously in a white cotton towel and still stuffed into a ragged old backpack. Camilla's candle, an irreplaceable link between the once great and important ancient tradition of Vesta worship and the modern world.

I unwrapped it, noticed a slight sweet fragrance, and held it in both my hands with newfound awe and respect. When last I saw it, I knew nothing of the Vesta tradition. I knew even less about marriage and family life. Now I knew a great deal about both.

For the first time, I noticed how heavy it really was and how the white glass of the candle holder resembled the white folds of a Vestal's robes. I noticed the deep amber color of the wax and the imperfect way it sat in the container, and realized the Vestal candle was hand-crafted, not manufactured: it was pure beeswax poured into an antique milk-glass bowl.

I had learned in university that pure yellow beeswax was used in candle-making by the ancient Romans, not only because of its availability but also because it was believed to be naturally pure in spirit, like Vesta herself. As a Vestal, Camilla had clearly tended to every detail. I felt a pang of guilt and foolishness. How had I not shown this item the reverence it warranted? How had I not realized what it meant?

As if it weren't bad enough that the Vestal temple and tradition had lain buried for centuries, it then had to endure the disrespect I had shown the last spark of its fire by leaving the Vestal candle buried for two decades under boxes, old clothes, forgotten files and pink flamingo lawn decorations.

A Risky Revelation

After I ransacked my parents' basement and found Camilla's candle, I thought about telling Don the story of my meeting with her in Rome. But imagining how that conversation might go gave me an instant stomach ache.

Don and I came from very different religious backgrounds. Although my grandmother was Roman Catholic and I grew up around Catholicism (I still have her old wooden rosary somewhere), I was raised in an atheist home. My parents had respect for other people's religions, so long as their ideology didn't hurt or subordinate anyone or anything, and wasn't being "shoved down our throats."

I remember an occasion in my youth when the Jehovah Witnesses came to our house. It was a cold winter night and my mom opened the front door: standing on our step were two men dressed in identical dark clothes, with a small, shivering girl standing between them.

My mom put her hands on her hips. "If you think dragging that poor frozen girl around is going to get me to sign up, you're wrong," she said. "Now go home, warm up her ears and put her to bed. It's a school night, for Christ's sake."

Don's religious background was radically different. He was brought up as a devout Christian and attended a cult-like church, complete with miracles, faith healings, raising of hands, faintings, talking in tongues and "end times" prophecies.

His childhood was spent in fervent, panicked prayer and the terrifying threat of burning in hell on account of his natural skepticism and tendency to ask the pastor inconvenient questions that he couldn't answer.

He had spent his youth trying to please his family and church leaders by doing overseas missionary work, teaching Sunday school and leading youth groups. Like so many people who experience such fundamentalism as a child, he rejected his religion, and all religion, as an adult. By comparison, I was an easygoing atheist. He was a militant one.

Both of us were raised in Canada's version of the Bible Belt, and it was in part my atheist background that had attracted him to me in the first place. I was the first nonreligious girl he had ever dated and I knew he liked that about me.

What would he say if I now hit him up with my spiritual enlightenment? What would he say if I started about a goddess named Vesta and how I met the last of twenty years ago in Rome?

He'd say, "You're losing it, Deb." He'd say, "I don't want my son hearing this bullshit, so keep it to yourself." He'd ask, "What's next? Midnight drum-beating circles in the forest? Dancing naked under a full moon? Giving ten percent of our salary to some cult leader who drives a Bugatti?" I could picture his expression and it made my stomach churn.

Yet god-talk wasn't completely absent from our home. Where other kids grew up hearing fairy tales, our kid grew up hearing legends from ancient mythology. Instead of listening to the Three Little Pigs or Jack and the Beanstalk, he would lie in bed and listen wide-eyed to the adventures of Greco-Roman gods, goddesses, demi-gods and heroes.

One of his favorite stories was that of Persephone, the beautiful daughter of Zeus and the harvest-goddess Demeter, who was kidnapped by Hades, the god of the underworld. Her mother searched the earth looking for her, neglecting her duties until the grain wilted and the humans starved.

Eventually, Hades and Demeter reached an agreement – Persephone would live with her mother on earth for part of the year and with Hades in the underworld for the other part of the year. When she is on earth, her mother is happy and the crops grow. That is summer. When she is in the underworld, her mother grieves and the crops die. That is winter.

Or the story of Pan who boasted that he could play music on his pipes that would rival the music of the great Apollo, the pretty-boy god who had his heart broken by Vesta herself when she turned down his marriage proposal. Pan was a cross between a man and a goat. He had horns, cloven feet and a spiked tail, and was the figure from which the Christians constructed their idea of the Devil.

Or the story of Eris, goddess of strife and argument, who was left off the guest list of a big wedding. Out of spite, she threw an apple with the words *For the Fairest Woman of All* into a crowd that included the goddesses Athena, Hera and Aphrodite. In so doing, Eris set off a sequence of cat-fights and events that would lead to the Trojan War. And she wondered why she had been left off the guest list.

Or the story of the Greek hero Achilles who fought in the same Trojan War. His mother had dipped him as a newborn baby into the River Styx, the river that flowed between the living world and the underworld, making him invincible. He had only one vulnerability – his Achilles' heel.

When his mother dipped him into the Styx, she had held him by his heel which therefore remained dry and powerless. After fighting in countless battles and remaining unwounded, Achilles was killed when a wayward arrow struck his heel.

It wasn't just my son who loved to hear about this rich Greco-Roman tradition and how it was still alive and well in our culture. Don enjoyed it, too. He'd lean on the doorway to our son's room at bed-time and listen to me tell the stories. Because of this, I knew that he would be open to hearing the story of Vesta and that he would like it.

But I wanted to do more than just tell the story of Vesta. I wanted to tell him how she had touched me on a personal, spiritual level. I wanted to embrace her tradition in our home and see whether her presence could keep me in the headspace and heartspace where, for the first time, I was completely happy and at peace with where I was in life.

Would Don be open to that? I thought not. I certainly couldn't risk dumping it all in his atheist lap and expecting him to sign up on the spot. I had to prove to him that my newfound faith could make our marriage stronger and our home a happier place.

And I suppose I still had to prove it to myself, too. My "spiritual awakening" had been a sudden, all-at-once experience. Although it felt authentic to the bone, I wanted to know that it wasn't a passing phase. That would require time and testing. It would also require some redecorating.

The Lararium

Long before the Temple of Vesta was built in the Roman Forum and her eternal flame became part of Roman state religion (which was believed to have happened in the 8th or 7th century BCE), the Vesta tradition was widespread and was an integral part of private Roman belief and household worship.

Symbolized by a flame and believed to be present in the home's burning fireplace, Vesta was the goddess of the home and the hearth. In Latin, the word "hearth" means focus. To devotees of Vesta, home was a sacred place. It was the focus of life. This was true of women who tended to the home and to their men who might be gone for years on military campaign.

The Flamma Vesta reminded men that their focus, their family, was waiting for them upon their return. They prayed to Vesta to protect their family in their absence. At the same time, wives and children prayed to Vesta that husbands and fathers would return safely home.

Each Roman home had a shrine or family altar, called a lararium, upon which a candle or an oil lamp would burn to symbolize Vesta. There might also be a statue of the goddess, but more often than not a simple flame represented her presence. This was the center of family worship and was located near the entrance of the home to bless the comings and goings of family members.

In addition to a flame and possibly a statue of Vesta, the lararium might also include small carved figures made of wood or marble that represented each living family member – mother, father, children – as well as deceased ancestors. These would be placed around Vesta, at her feet.

If you have ever seen Ridley Scott's movie *Gladiator*, there is a poignant scene about thirty minutes into the film where the protagonist Maximus (played by Russell Crowe), prays for his family at such an altar. He kneels before a lararium and holds two small carved figures that represent his wife and son.

A statue of Vesta can be seen standing in the middle of the altar, robed and veiled, surrounded by burning candles that represent her sacred fire.

Rather than risking a bare-all spiritual revelation to Don, I decided to make a family lararium of our own and see whether he would ask about it. I figured that might be a good segue into the conversation and ease him into the idea.

I bought a tall, narrow glass table and placed it in the foyer to our home, below a reproduction painting of a 1st century CE Roman wall fresco from Herculaneum, to create an elegant lararium altar.

Then, I placed Camilla's candle, the Flamma Vesta, in the middle of the altar. Beside it, I set a small glass bottle of wine and a ceramic plate, both of which were for offerings. I added a few more meaningful items: a rock from a desert vacation, a plaster cast of our son's hand, dried flower petals from my wedding bouquet and a little ceramic owl from my mom and dad.

Being an avid collector of antiques and historical prints, I searched for Vestal antiques to add to my collection and I placed these on the lararium as well: a bronze statue of the goddess, an 18th century CE print of the Temple of Vesta and an ancient 3rd century BCE silver denarius struck with the inscription VESTA MATER (Mother Vesta) and showing a lovely image of the goddess offering a libation over a lighted altar at the temple.

To Don, it was just Roman-themed home décor, which was nothing unusual for our house. Trinkets. He never paid much attention to furniture. He did, however, pay great attention to the new wife that was apparently delivered with the new table.

The truth is, the lararium didn't just look good. It did good, too. Its presence served as a visual reminder that kept me in line. Every morning when Don went to work, it was there to remind me to kiss him, to say kind words in parting, to smile. I would make a point of walking him to the door and saying good-bye to him, and I prompted our son to do the same.

Every evening when he came home, the lararium was there waiting for him to come through the door and reminding me to meet him there. I would unlock the door and open it so that he didn't have to fish through his pockets for his house key or fight with the lock while standing outside in the cold trying to juggle his lunch box and work papers and cell phone.

Soon, my son joined me at the door to welcome his dad home without being prompted to do so. He'd automatically put down his toys or comic book and dash to the doorway with genuine excitement. Both of us welcomed Don home with a smile and warmth, as if we couldn't wait for him to come home, as if there were no more important, loved or anticipated person on the planet.

Don's face said it all. He felt like a king. Why? Because we were taking a whopping thirty seconds out of our day to meet him at the door. "This is my favorite part of the day," he'd say.

And I'd try not to burst into tears with regret and self-loathing for the years I couldn't have been bothered to give him those thirty seconds.

For those times he'd come through the door, dropping his keys or paperwork or phone in the process, and walk into a house where nobody seemed to notice he'd been gone for twelve or fourteen hours. For those times I couldn't have been bothered to peek my head around the corner to say 'hi' or stop stirring the pot on the stove or turn around from my computer.

I guess I'm lucky he kept coming home at all.

CHAPTER IV

Revelations and Roots

Just as a candle cannot burn without fire, men cannot live without a spiritual life.
  - Buddha, Sage, Between 6th & 4th Centuries BCE

Familiarity breeds contempt, while rarity wins admiration.
  - Apuleius, Latin Poet, 125 – 180 CE

Lighting (and Lightening) Up

In the weeks after our return from Las Vegas, I found that I was happier, more relaxed and flexible, more positive. It was like I had taken the biggest, deepest breath of my life and let it all out.

My patience and perspective had grown. I had stopped feeling sorry for myself and started feeling gratitude, reverence and joy for the home I had and for those I shared it with. The presence of the family altar and Camilla's Vestal candle – even though I hadn't yet renewed its flame – was already lighting a new path for me.

The dynamics in my marriage and family life had palpably changed. I realized how much the quality of our home life centered around my attitude and behavior. When I was happier, more content and able to feel fulfilled without having to prove anything, my husband and son smiled more, laughed more, loved more. Everyone was relaxed. Everyone was enjoying each other.

Although Don had always been a great husband, he upped his efforts even more. I would have to race him to clean off the table or help our son with his homework. He'd run me baths and flirt with me non-stop.

He'd surprise us with family trips to museums, antique bookshops, waterparks, sci-fi expos and comic conventions for our superhero-obsessed son. He'd start random countdowns: "15, 14, 13, 12, 11..." during dinner or family movies, and we'd have to race to the car to get there by "0" if we wanted to go for ice-cream.

He swept us, a family of stargazers, off our feet for a whirlwind trip to the Kitt Peak National Observatory in Tucson, Arizona where we gazed into deep space through high-powered telescopes to see nebulae, star clusters, galaxies and the great red spot on Jupiter.

If I'd seen my family from the outside, I'd probably have gagged on the nauseating happiness. From the inside, however, it was fabulous.

One evening during supper – it was a rare occasion that we were actually sitting at the table as a family – Don mentioned the lararium as if he hadn't noticed it before. Which he probably hadn't.

"How long has that glass table been in the foyer?" he asked.

"Since we got back from Vegas," I said, smiling. "How astute of you to notice."

Filled with a sudden burst of courage – or maybe it was just that second glass of wine – I saw an opening and I went for it. I came clean. I told him and our son everything.

I told them about my trip to the Roman Forum and the Temple of Vesta over twenty years earlier. About Camilla and how she and the Vestals before her had kept the Flame of Vesta burning in secret through the generations and how she had passed that secret down to me. How the candle on the glass table in our foyer held the Flamma Vesta.

I told them about Vesta. About how she was the goddess of the family hearth and home, how her simple faith could be traced back to prehistory when humans instinctually worshipped fire, and how it had been a beloved, widespread tradition until it was violently suppressed by the new religion on the block, Christianity.

I told them about how I had been privately pressure-testing the Vesta tradition in my life – after all, if its philosophy and practices could make *me* a happier and more peaceful person, there must be something to it, right?

I gushed about the presence of Vesta's sacred fire in every ancient home, and how families would make an offering to her before and after every meal. This was never an animal – Vesta was a bloodless religion – but was instead salted flour, wine or olive oil sprinkled into her flame.

I told them that whenever someone today lights a candle at a table, whether it's for a Christmas supper, a family meal or a romantic dinner, that person is performing a Vestal ritual. I told them that the very concept of the eternal flame comes from the Vesta tradition.

And then I waited, ready to top up my glass of wine if necessary. If they looked at me weird or made fun of me or patronized me.

"So that's how you got that old candle?" asked our son. "Wow, mom, you're like a female Indiana Jones."

"Yeah, just like," I said.

"And that's what this change has been all about?" Don asked. "You know I hate the fluffy spiritual stuff, but this is pretty amazing. Why haven't you ever told us this story?"

"I don't know," I said. "I thought you'd think I was crazy."

"I know you're crazy," he said, "so relax." Then he asked a question that almost make me choke on my bread. "Was Vesta for men, too?"

"Absolutely," I said. "Men in the ancient world had no hang-ups about honoring a goddess. Vesta was a comfort to them, a protector of their home and family, especially when they were away. They would look to her for guidance when they were troubled or needed advice, especially since her tradition included ancestor worship."

"Ancestor worship?"

I explained how the Romans felt deeply connected to their ancestors and family lines. Masks and figures of their grandparents, great-grandparents and beyond were kept on or around the lararium, near the Flame of Vesta. When a man had a problem, he would look to Vesta and to his ancestors for guidance.

Maybe it's a man thing, but for some reason this particular part of the Vesta tradition seemed to resonate more with Don than with me.

"Most guys nowadays don't even know the names of their great-grandfathers," he said. "It's no wonder families are falling apart. There's no pride in keeping them together. There's no sense of duty or of carrying on your family name."

He was right about that. In my practice, I had seen many men (and women) who didn't seem to take the concept of family very seriously. They certainly didn't seem to fight very hard for it. Many of them seemed to think it would be easier – or perhaps just more exciting – to begin a brand new family than to repair or renew the one they already had.

"When a man knows his family heritage, he knows where he comes from," he said, "and who he is. He's part of something bigger. It gives a guy a sense of responsibility, too. This is your family and you stay and fight for it, protect it, no matter what."

Suddenly, Don pushed his chair from the table. He went downstairs and, after rummaging around for a while, came back up carrying a beat-up old wrench and a rectangular hand-made wooden box.

He passed the box to our son. "This is the only thing I asked for when my grandfather – your great-grandfather Macleod – died," he said. "It's a collection of old lighters that he put into this box…he made it with his own hands." He set the wrench on the table. "Your other great-grandfather built Boeing airplanes. This is one of his tools he gave me on our last visit."

"These are cool," said our son. "Can we put these on the lararium?"

"Sure."

You see, with Don it's all about evidence. Since we had returned from Vegas, he had seen the proof that this simple "spirituality of the home" could make a difference in our home. In a jaw-dropping, out-of-character moment, he even admitted that he missed the comfort of certain rituals in his life – they had always given him focus.

Most especially, though, he liked the fact that the Vesta tradition truly put family first. That was different than his experience with religion, which ordered a man to put a god and the church before his own family.

His reaction was nothing like I thought it would be. I thought he'd look down his nose at my story about Camilla and my fledgling spiritual side, but instead he let me see that he too was missing that aspect of life. Wow, you think you know someone.

My son piped up. "So what are we waiting for? Let's go light the candle."

"We can't," I said. "I met Camilla on March 1st, which was no coincidence. That was the Roman new year, the day that Vesta's fire was renewed in the temple. So cool your heels. I'd like to wait until then."

"That's a month away," he said. "I can't wait that long."

"I'm happy that you're so excited about it," I grinned. I pointed to the candle that was burning on the kitchen table. "I'll tell you what. Until then, let's use this regular candle at suppertime, and if you want, you can be the guy in charge of making an offering before we eat."

"Like throwing food into it?

"I don't know about *throwing*, but sprinkling some flour or oil into the flame would be fun, wouldn't it?"

"Throwing would be more fun," he shrugged, "but sprinkling will do."

Finding Our Roots

In the wake of my suppertime revelation about Camilla and the Flamma Vesta, I was surprised by how much Don began to talk about his family roots and how much our son asked about them. The ancient tradition of ancestor worship really seemed to strike a chord with them.

I deliberately stepped back from this. I loved that they were getting into the Vesta tradition, but I didn't want to push it on them. Their genuine interest was a bonus: I would have been content with their simply humoring me and letting me light my candles in snicker-free peace.

After a while, I joined the action. I began to collect old photographs of my and Don's ancestors. I showed our son time-worn black and white photographs of his great-grandparents on my side, Olga and Joseph, and his great-great-grandparents, Pearl and Michael. I let him look into their faces and I asked him to imagine what their voices might have sounded like. I framed their pictures and placed them on the lararium, so that their presence was again in the world.

I told my son what I knew about these people, his ancestors, who lived not so long ago. How Olga made the best pedaheh (perogies). How Joseph caught the biggest trout on record in Manitoba. How Pearl had a mischievous sense of humor.

How Michael, when he first came to Canada from the Ukraine, cut ice from a frozen lake and hauled the massive blocks from door to door, selling them to people in the days before refrigeration. In those days, ice covered in sawdust was the only way to prevent food from spoiling. It was also the only way for Michael to make enough money to feed his family for the first year they spent in their new country.

I would say, "Maybe you got your sense of humor from your great-great-grandmother. Maybe you get your industriousness from your great-great grandfather." Then I would make pedaheh, using my grandmother's recipe.

We'd invite my parents over and casually prompt them to tell stories about their childhoods and the early years of their marriage. I was surprised by how much I didn't know. They had always been doting grandparents, but had never really shared the details of their own rich history. Life gets busy and such things seem to loose their relevance.

Yet our son was fascinated by it. To be sure, he has a love of history in his blood. But there was more to it. He seemed to sense that when he was learning about these people, he was learning about himself.

While the goal may have been to give our son a sense of having deep family roots, I found that I too was gaining a new appreciation for my parents. I'm ashamed to admit it, but there were times when I'd let their calls go to voicemail or break a dinner date because I was too busy. I stopped doing that. I started answering each and every call as if it might be the last time I ever spoke to them. I sat and enjoyed a cup of tea with them and didn't stare at the clock.

By choosing to live like this, I'm showing my son how to treat me when I'm older. That's important, since the way he treats me will show his children how to treat him. I want his kids to respect him, to care for him, to be patient with him as he ages and to value what he has to say and offer as long as he lives.

Children don't learn these lessons and behaviors by accident or instinct. If they don't see them in action, if they don't live with them, they don't do them.

Seeing Things in a New Light

It seemed a bit strange to see those time-worn black and white pictures on the lararium, those faces from the past that were at once so distant and so close. "Family" that was so unfamiliar and so familiar at the same time.

Don and our son began to research the family tree in a more serious way. The more we learned about our ancestors, the more we learned about our current family. The more fascinated we became with their histories, the more fascinated we became with the history we were making as a family. The past made us see the present in a new light.

Seeing something "in a new light" is important. It's a big part of what Vesta and my newfound faith was helping me to do. I realized that. And it reminded me of something that happened during an art history class that I took in my first year of university.

The professor was talking about a modern artist and his team who spent a dark night wrapping a long-defunct bridge – one that ran parallel to a newer and functioning bridge – in a massive, colorful tarp. The next morning, commuters traveling on the newer bridge were pulled over and asked for their thoughts.

Of course, most people were shocked by the sight of a giant pink-tarped bridge; however, what *really* surprised people was the fact that, over the years, they had completely forgotten the old bridge was even there.

Seeing it in a new light – wrapped in an eye-catching tarp instead of just blending into the background of a mindless morning commute – brought back memories of traveling over the bridge, fishing off it, walking across it with a sweetheart.

The creator of this project was using an artistic device called ostranenie, or defamiliarization, which was coined by the Russian writer Viktor Shlovsky. Its purpose is to present what is familiar, perhaps too familiar (since familiarity breeds contempt, as they say), and present it in a way that is unfamiliar.

When a person's perspective changes, she sees the world in a new way. She has a new experience with something that may be very old to her.

There is a scene in the film *Dead Poets Society* where Robin Williams's character – a professor – suddenly stands on his desk during a lecture and then instructs his students to stand on their desks as well. His purpose is to challenge them to look at things in a different way. To see the ordinary in an extra-ordinary way.

In so doing, he is using the concept of defamiliarization. Their classroom, so familiar and expected, transforms into a new space when seen from a new perspective or when seen in an uncommon or unexpected way. It's why even a familiar street can seem so different, even disorientingly different, at night than it does during the day.

As academic as it sounds, I started to use this artistic device in my own life. I wanted to see my life, my home, my family from the top of my desk instead of just from behind it. I wanted to experience and appreciate it in a new way. So I started to make little changes.

When I went grocery shopping, I challenged myself to buy flatbread instead of bread, Romaine lettuce instead of iceberg and sorbet instead of ice cream. Little things. Yet making these small changes made me realize how habitual many of my actions and choices were. I was on automatic pilot so much of the time, tossing the same items week after week into the cart.

My family noticed everything. My son would say, "This ice cream is delicious!" while Don would say, "I really like sandwiches like this." It sounds so trivial, yet the taste of something new, the presentation of food in an unfamiliar way, made all the difference.

I went further and dressed up the kitchen table with an elegant table cloth as well as new plates, glassware and cutlery. I indulged in cloth napkins with marble napkin rings. I set Vestal candles in the center of the table, along with a vase of fresh flowers, a wooden pepper mill and a glass bottle of olive oil.

Family mealtime became family mealtime. No more eating from the pot while our son chowed down in front of the television and Don shoved whatever I had made into his mouth while simultaneously sending out the last of his work email. We ate by candlelight, talking and laughing our faces off, while Frank Sinatra sang quietly in the background.

I branched out, aiming for sensory overload as a way to constantly remind myself – or more accurately to stimulate myself – to experience the familiar in an unfamiliar way. I burned sweet-smelling incense and changed my laundry soap. I changed the color of my walls and replaced some artwork. I put new cushions on the sofa. I bought a few exotic houseplants. Instead of having a shower before bedtime, I indulged in a hot milk bath complete with candles on the side of the tub and Classical music.

I changed the master bedroom, too, something that had a rather dramatic effect on what went on in there, I am happy to report. The sterile blinds went into the dumpster, usurped by heavier, sexier drapes that blocked out the lights and hung elegantly to the floor. The worn cotton sheets went into the bin, replaced by luxurious linen. The glaring white lightbulbs in our bedside lamps were tossed in favor of a warmer, softer glow. The experience of "going to bed" went from predictable to passionate. Our utilitarian bedroom became a sensual sanctuary.

These little changes in perspective, these little changes in what I saw, smelled, tasted and felt renewed the experience of home. It renewed the experience of family life. It kept me in the mindset where, day after day, my surroundings stimulated me to say, "I love this place. I love these people. I love my life."

Challenging myself to see my life, family and home in a new light gave me a new appreciation for them. I now see them as they are, not as I expect them to be. I am mindful that every moment, as banal and familiar as it seems, is actually a fascinating experience that the universe has given me. I am grateful for each moment I have on this earth with the people I love. After all, I've lived long enough to know that the next moment might take them away.

Each of us is an artist and a creator. We are creating our own work of art – our life. It will be finished on the day we die. Until then, we are free to cover the canvas with whatever colors and subjects we want.

Just remember to shine the light differently on the canvas now and then. Change the brushstrokes, or throw away the brushes altogether and get your hands dirty. Close your eyes and throw some color onto it. Let the cat walk over it. Whatever.

I remember a male student in my art history class laughed out loud at the example of the pink-tarped bridge. "That's not art," he said. "I could have done that."

"But you didn't," said the professor, "and that's why we're talking about this artist and not about you."

It's easy to criticize and to make excuses. When I worked as a divorce mediator, I saw that kind of thing all the time: people who were bored with their partners and home lives, or who were stuck in a depressing, going-nowhere cycle of conflict or apathy. They existed within the bleak familiarity of one prevailing emotion – unhappiness.

And they did nothing to change it. If someone challenged them to get up and stand on their desk, they'd remain seated. Why? Who knows. Fear. Stubbornness. Pride. Indifference. Laziness. Close-mindedness.

The scary thing is, that kind of bleakness can sneak up on a person. You need to constantly be aware of it, to be on guard for it. You need to shine a bright light into the dark spaces where it hides and gains the strength it needs to take you down, once and for all.

I stayed on guard against that bleakness by trying to see, smell, taste and feel my life in a different way, on a daily basis. And by doing that, new light was shed on what could have all too easily become a very dark place.

CHAPTER V

Reigniting the Flamma Vesta

Vesta, you have gained an everlasting abode and highest honor: glorious is your portion and your right. Come and dwell in this house in friendship together.
- Homeric Hymn to Vesta, 7th to 4th Century BCE

To Vesta, who dwellest amidst great fire's eternal flame; Eternal, ever florid queen, laughing and blessed, accept these rites and needful good inspire.
- Orphic Hymn to Vesta, 3rd Century BCE to 2nd Century CE

As March 1st drew nearer, the significance of relighting the Vestal candle grew bigger in my mind. It had been ceremoniously renewed every year for centuries – albeit secretly so – and I wondered about what measures Camilla and other Vestals had taken to sustain the sacred flame. What had they done to prevent such a precious artefact from melting away into nonexistence?

I knew I had to find a way to preserve the flame; however, I wanted to do more than just preserve it. I also wanted to spread Vesta's fire, just as the ancient Vestals used to do by distributing the sacred flame to women who wished to burn it in their own homes.

At first, my idea was to simply light new candles with the flame of Camilla's candle and spread the flame that way; however, I wanted something more substantial. There was only one solution that I could think of.

In addition to lighting the wicks of new candles with the Flame of Vesta, I would also blend some of the melted wax from Camilla's Vestal candle with the wax from new candles. It was the most genuine way of spreading the Flamma Vesta while making the original Vestal candle last as long as possible. Plus, I knew that Camilla had handmade her candle and I felt an obligation to carry on her tradition as closely as possible.

There was just one problem. This required that I learn how to make handcrafted candles. Now to put this into perspective, I must tell you that from elementary school to law school, I was an A student. I never struggled in school...with the exception of one class in junior high. I tremble at the very memory. Home Economics.

Back when I was in junior high, Home Economics was probably more gender-biased than it is now. It used to be for female students only, where girls were taught to cook, sew and do various "handicrafts."

It was the only class that I ever failed in my academic career. If we were making cookies, I started an oven fire. If we were sewing a shirt, mine was inside out and completely unrecognizable as any kind of garment.

I remember one class where we were learning to seal jars for canning food. Seriously, this was the most confusing, terrifying concept I had ever heard of. To this day it doesn't make sense. Anyway, I think the general goal was to melt paraffin wax and use it to seal the jars. I remember the teacher looking right at me as she was describing the process.

"This is melted wax, Debra. It is very hot. Do you know what that means?"

"It means it will burn our skin."

"Very good."

But knowing a thing and avoiding a thing are two different things. Of course I broke my jar. Of course I spilled the wax. Of course I burned myself and managed to pour wax onto my shoes.

The next day, my mother went to the principal's office where she had a rather heated conversation with him. After that, I had the distinction of being the first girl in my school to drop out of Home Economics and sign up for Shop Class. Looking back, I'm not sure about my mom's logic. "Let's get her away from ovens and hot wax, and put circular saws and power drills in her hands."

My point is, I'd never been crafty. At all. So when I told my family that I was going to make hand poured candles, I received tight little smiles back in response.

"Good luck with that," they said.

I would catch my husband and my son exchanging glances, as if to say, "She's going to burn the house down, you know." Don quietly replaced the old fire detectors in our house with new ones. A fire extinguisher miraculously appeared under the kitchen sink.

Trial by Fire

If anything were ever a process of trial and error – sometimes a scalding process – it was my idea to become a master candle maker in my own kitchen.

We ordered supper in for two weeks straight as the kitchen became a candle-making shop. The microwave and toaster went onto the floor as the countertops were taken over with pour pots, basins, thermometers, bags of wax, a plethora of various candle containers and packages of wicks.

I experimented with different waxes: paraffin wax, soy wax, paraffin-soy blends, bleached beeswax, until I learned how each one melted, poured and cured in various types of containers. I experimented with different wicks: cored wicks, flat braided wicks, until I learned how each had a distinct capillary action and burn rate.

I experimented with combinations: this type of wax with that type of wick, and then that type of wax with this type of wick. I spilled hot wax over the counters and stovetop, down the cupboards, into drawers and across the floor.

And I burned myself. A lot.

I remember one occasion when I was hard at work and my son sauntered into the kitchen. He stared at me for a moment, as though he was watching a witch at a bubbling cauldron, and then held up a piece of paper. Upon it was a picture of a woman in a red dress with a long, flowing white veil.

"This is the superhero Vesta," he said, "from Marvel Comics. She appeared in Thor number 301." He looked back at the page and the corner of his lip lifted in disapproval. "They've got her wrong," he said. Without another word, he strolled out of the kitchen.

On another occasion, Don was sitting at the table looking at this laptop as I banged and clanged in the kitchen.

"Did you know that there's an asteroid named Vesta? It's called 4 Vesta. It has minor-planet designation and it's one of the largest asteroids in the solar system…in the asteroid belt between Jupiter and Mars."

I stopped pouring wax and looked at him. "No, I didn't know that."

"They named it Vesta because it's the brightest asteroid visible from Earth," he continued. He looked up from the computer. "It says here that Vesta was at its brightest magnitude in 1989."

"You're lying."

"Isn't that the year you met Camilla?"

"Yes, it is."

"Wow, what are the odds," he said.

A Spark of Simplicity

At first, I had been focused on creating elaborate candles, some brightly colored, some sculpted, some scented with essential oils and others glazed with sand. I poured them into colored and frosted containers of all shapes and sizes. And then I sat fuming on the floor when they didn't look like the amazing works of modern art that I had wanted them to be.

I then decided that a "pure" look – similar to Catholic liturgical candles – was better, so I switched to pure white soy wax and bleached white beeswax. And then I again sat fuming on the floor when they looked too sterile and contrived.

I was having one such floor temper-tantrum when the cat crawled onto my lap. He looked up at me as if to say, 'Relax woman, and give me a piece of salami.' I thought of the feral cats in the Roman Forum, the cats Camilla had seemed to know by name. My thoughts turned to her Vestal candle and the way the flame had been passed down to her, to me.

The dark amber beeswax of the Vestal candle was obviously very old, possibly centuries old. It had likely nourished the sacred flame for generations, and had been preserved by pouring it from large vessels to smaller ones as it burned and melted.

I assumed it was Camilla who had poured this beeswax into the milk-glass container that now housed it and the sacred flame. Although she had clearly been something of a glamor girl and the milk-glass vessel was a stylish choice, Camilla had done nothing to glam-up the actual beeswax – the old, dark amber was, to be honest, neither pretty nor pristine.

So I abandoned my vision of pretty or pristine Vestal candles. As I packed the dyes and bleached waxes into the cupboard, I found a pail of honey from the local farmer's market. It came from an apiary just outside of town, so I called the number on the lid to see if I could buy pure beeswax from their hives.

Within an hour, I was driving home with slabs of beeswax taking up the back seat, squishing the dog and making the air inside my car smell sweet. The amber color of this new beeswax was lighter than the old beeswax, but it was the natural choice.

Next, I decided to use a wooden wick – one that produced a distinct crackle when it burned – to animate the flame. The ancients believed that a crackle in Vesta's fire brought good fortune, as if the goddess herself were speaking or laughing. Camilla's Vestal candle contained a cotton wick; however, I think she'd approve of this single upgrade. In fact, I suspect she would have chosen a wooden wick had they been more widely available when she made her candle.

Finally, I chose a modest but elegant round, clear-glass votive to house the new candles and the Flamma Vesta. The simplicity and transparency of this container would offer the cleanest, clearest view of the burning flame within. It also reflected the circular shape of the Temple of Vesta as well as Camilla's original Vestal candle.

Catching Fire

When March 1st finally arrived, I had the house to myself. The act of renewing the Flamma Vesta was something that I wanted to do in peace and privacy.

Alone in a quiet house, I began the process by melting a large pot of beeswax on the stove, arranging my candle-making supplies and lining up the votives and wicks. All seemed set.

But how to relight the sacred fire of Vesta after decades in the dark? How to reawaken her slumbering spirit within the ancient amber beeswax? I thought about using a lighter, but that seemed somehow soulless.

In antiquity, Vesta's sacred fire would have been renewed using an iron fire-striker and flint. Striking these together created a spark which was then fanned into a flame.

Wanting to blend Old World and New World elements into this modern renewal, I had found at auction an authentic 1st century CE iron fire-striker of the type used to renew Vesta's fire in the temple. It was a lovely specimen that boasted a scroll design that, to me, looked a lot like a flame.

Instead of using flint, however, I chose to use something more modern, something that had meaning to me. After my grandfather had passed away, I had taken a small box of odds and ends from his and my grandmother's cabin, where I had spent every summer of my childhood. These trinkets had sentimental value only. An old jackknife. A fishing hook my grandpa made. A grocery list written in my grandma's handwriting.

And a vintage box of wooden strike-anywhere matches. My grandfather had started more fires than I could remember with the matches from this very box. The cabin would be cold in the morning – Canadian summer nights are chilly – and my sister and I would stay huddled under the bedcovers until he had started a fire in the old wood stove.

Within minutes, the loud crackles and snaps of the firewood would echo within the log walls. The heat from the fire would move and roll, like warm ocean waves, into each tiny room. Soon, my sister and I would be out of bed and the cabin would be full of chatter, laughter and the smell of coffee.

I took one match out of the battered old box. To my mind, it had called Vesta many times to the cabin in my childhood. It could do the same here and now.

I held Camilla's Vestal candle in both of my hands. It was cool to the touch, and I could feel the folds of the vintage milk-glass pressing against my palm and the back of my fingers. The white glass drapery of the bowl surrounded and cradled the ancient amber beeswax within, like a white Vestal robe embracing a priestess. I was struck again by how heavy it was.

I set the Vestal candle on the lararium and then gently trimmed the tip of the singed cotton wick to prepare it for its fiery renewal.

I struck the wooden match against the iron fire-striker and the Flamma Vesta reignited itself instantly – far faster and fuller than I had expected – and flared up high into a thick, strong flame that licked the side of the milk glass, quickly charring the inside of the rim and leaving a trail of black soot on the amber beeswax, before finally settling into a regular, relaxed flame.

I had the sense that the flame wasn't just being reignited or renewed, it was being resuscitated. It was like a breathless creature who at first gasps desperately for air and life and then, once realizing its lungs are once again full, relaxes and begins to breathe more regularly.

For the first time in over two decades, I was in the presence of the true Flamma Vesta. I looked into the flame, felt its heat and sensed a sacredness filling the space around me.

I thought about everything this simple faith had brought to my life and my home, and then dipped my fingers into a shallow bowl of olive oil and sprinkled it onto the flame as an offering of gratitude.

Again, the Flamma Vesta flared up as if in hunger. It flickered for a moment as it consumed the offering and then settled into a slow-burning flame, sated and sure.

I spent a long time in quiet reflection as Camilla's candle burned. I don't know how much time had passed when, suddenly, I became aware of how much wax had pooled around the base of the wick.

Shaking off my reverie, I gently scooped a pool of melted beeswax from the Vestal candle and put it into the pot of melting beeswax on my stove. I poured the melted wax – new beeswax with a splash of sacred old beeswax – into each votive and then lowered a splayed wooden wick into the center of the blend.

After the new candles had partly cured, I transferred the Flamma Vesta from Camilla's candle to each of the new candles, letting each wooden wick burn into a strong flame before extinguishing it.

In this way, I created new Vestal candles from the old. It would now be possible to gift the sacred flame to women who wanted to burn it in their home, as was the custom in antiquity. For the first time in a long time, Vesta's fire could spread.

I sprinkled another offering of olive oil into the flame and was about to extinguish it – knowing that it would be another year until I saw it burn again – when Don and our son arrived home.

Apparently our son was adamant that he wanted to see Camilla's candle in action. Judging by his expression, though, it didn't live up to his lofty expectations. After all the hype and build-up, I think he half-expected a hologram of the white-robed goddess Vesta to spring out of the candle, just as Princess Leia had sprung out of R2-D2. When that didn't happen, he disappeared downstairs to play video games.

Don was slightly more interested. "So, your candle fired right up, did it?"

"Yes," I said. "And you didn't have to come home early. The house didn't catch on fire."

"I never doubted you for a moment," he said unconvincingly, then added, "how are you going to keep this flame burning for whole year?"

"I wasn't going to. I was just going to light it once a year and make new candles."

"But didn't Vesta's fire burn all year long in the temple?"

"Yes, but I don't see how that's possible," I thought for a moment. "Unless we got one of those long-burning oil lamps? Or one lit by ethanol, maybe?"

Don shook his head. "Can't leave those things unattended," he said. "As soon as your head was turned, Frosty would be setting his tail on fire with it. He'd be a moving torch."

He was right about that. The cat had a very fluffy tail and felt no higher calling than to dust household items with it, as though in cat-critique of my housekeeping. Notwithstanding the cat's tail, the idea of leaving a flame burning in our house, especially in our absence, was out of the question.

70

After centuries of continuous burning, and then centuries of lying dormant, it looked like an annual renewing ceremony was the best I could offer the Flamma Vesta.

The Flame and the Furnace

But then Don came up with an idea that I hated.

"I can start the pilot light with it," he said. " Then it will burn non-stop in the furnace."

I flashed him a look of disgust. "Seriously, Don? This flame burned for generations in the Temple of Vesta, in thousands of households. People prayed to it, worshipped it. You want it to burn in the basement of our bungalow?"

He shrugged. "Do you want to keep it burning or not?"

I thought about it. Was a furnace really so different than the hearths that heated ancient Roman homes? Was a furnace really so different than the wood stoves that heated old homes and cabins? The purpose and spirit were exactly the same, even if times had changed.

So I followed him downstairs with Camilla's candle, into the laundry room, around the corner to the furnace. He lifted the metal panel off and turned off the furnace to extinguish the pilot light, then patted the concrete floor for me to sit beside him.

"You can do the honors," he said.

"Do you see any spiders down there?" I asked. "Look behind the furnace."

"All clear."

I knelt beside him, first tilting a tapered candle into Camilla's Vestal candle until it caught fire, and then sliding the tip into the furnace, into the stream of natural gas.

"Are you sure this isn't going to blow up the house?" I asked.

"I'm sure," he said. "But shouldn't you be murmuring some Latin ceremonial chant right now? Or maybe taking your clothes off?"

I glared at him and he went quiet.

I heard a *whoosh* as the flame ignited. Don sat back and gestured to it. "There you go."

I stared at the blue flame. Despite the concrete floor of the basement, despite the old green covering of the furnace and its clunky metal innards, despite the unceremonious relighting, the Flamma Vesta burned strong and elegant.

I wondered what Camilla would think. Would she be offended by the idea of the sacred fire of Vesta burning in my bungalow? It wasn't the reverent relighting the flame deserved. But when I looked at the flame burning strong and bright in the furnace, it struck me that perhaps this March 1st, 2012 renewal ceremony-of-sorts wasn't all bad. It was simple, but it was sincere.

In antiquity, the presence of the Flamma Vesta in the family hearth essentially made each home a private, domestic Temple of Vesta.

In modernity, the presence of the Flamma Vesta in the family furnace can do precisely the same thing. It can make each home a sacred space blessed by the spirit of Vesta. My home was the first; however, I knew it was just the beginning. After all, it is the nature of fire – especially a sacred, eternal fire – to spread.

The Voice of New Vesta

A few nights later, my son and I were curled up on the couch in the living room, reading and chatting. It was a chilly night and we were snuggled under a blanket.

As he usually does on such nights, Don arranged a few logs of wood in the fireplace and started a fire. The fire began to hiss and crackle before finally spreading into a roar, sending waves of heat into the room and causing me to kick off the blanket.

"I started it with the flame from the furnace," said Don.

I put down my book and looked into the fire. The fire of New Vesta.

It was one thing to see the Flamma Vesta as a solitary flame in a candle, or even the furnace for that matter – those were lovely – but it was something else entirely to see it dancing and hear it crackling as a roaring fire. To feel its heat, almost too hot, against the skin. The flame had become a beautiful inspiration to me, elegant and eternal, but now I saw another element – its raging power.

I heard it, too. The roar, snaps and pops, the crackling as sparks flew out of the fire and flames licked the sides of the fireplace, climbed up the chimney and reached out of the metal screen. Don turned off the lights and we sat as a family in the fire-lit room as Vesta spoke in a voice as old as antiquity, as old as the human experience, as old as fire and the universe.

While we talked about schoolwork and books and movies and summer vacations, she talked about the millions of ancient families who offered oil to her, the empire she protected, the priestesses who lovingly tended to her fire and the beautiful temple that she once called home.

Home is something that Vesta knows a lot about.

Renewing her tradition in the modern home can carve out a space in the universe that you can call your own. A space where you, your spouse, your children, even your pets exist in a microcosm of the universal energy. A happy, loving, sacred space called home.

CHAPTER VI

Happiness and Heaven

Happiness resides not in possessions and not in gold. Happiness dwells in the soul.
- Democritus, Greek Philosopher, 460 – 370 BCE

A happy life does not come from external things: one draws from within, as from a spring.
- Plutarch, Roman Historian, 46 – 120 CE

Get Thee to a Nunnery

Following my visit to the Forum and my meeting with Camilla, and before attending university, I lived and worked in a small tourist resort town in the Canadian Rocky Mountains.

It was, and still is, common for young adults to spend a season or two here, skiing in the winter and enjoying the scenery in the summer, often saving money for school while working at one of the many hotels or restaurants. I was lucky enough to snag a better paying clerical job in the local hospital.

Not too far from the hospital there was a pretty Catholic church. A nun from the church spent a lot of time at the hospital in which I worked, comforting the sick and dying. A delightful and kind-hearted lady, Sister Maria was very well-liked among the staff, including myself, and she and I struck up a quick and easy friendship.

Sister Maria was about the same age as Camilla and it was perhaps one of those strange cosmic coincidences that I was to meet her only months after meeting Camilla. Although of the same generation, these women could not have been more different.

Where Camilla wore high Italian boots into her eighties, Sister Maria wore old-fashioned, worn-out ladies' loafers. Where Camilla's sure voice travelled across the expanse of the Forum, Sister Maria's voice was more self-conscious.

I had the sense that Camilla could have run a multinational corporation while bottle-feeding her son and browsing through a glossy lingerie magazine for something sexy to wear for her husband. Sister Maria came across as subordinate, even submissive, and I often wondered whether she had ever made an independent decision in her life.

Sister Maria and I spent quite a few lunches and coffee breaks together at work, and when she would ask me to attend a service at her church I was happy to do so. It seemed to please her. She lived in a two or three-bedroom apartment, I believe with another nun whom I never met, and I remember being invited to have tea there several times.

At the Forum, Camilla had spoken briefly about Catholic nuns and there were many questions I wanted to ask Sister Maria. I remember the afternoon I told her about my meeting with Camilla. We were sitting on a park bench watching a tourist try to coax a massive elk toward his small children so that he could take a picture. Superb parenting.

"I met the most amazing woman when I was in Rome," I told the sister. "She said that she was the last Vestal, and that the Catholic nunhood was based on the Vestal order of priestesses. Have you ever heard of that?"

It was a Jekyll and Hyde moment. The very instant I mentioned the words "Vestal priestess," the open-hearted, kind lady I knew disappeared and a close-minded stranger appeared.

"Christ the redeemer died on the cross for our sins. The only salvation is through him. The church has banished pagan witchcraft from the earth."

I might as well have said that Camilla and I had donned devil horns and sacrificed babies on the hearth of the temple. Sister Maria stood up and left.

I remember feeling shocked and confused. In my youth and naivety I had fully expected the sister to be interested in the remarkable experience I had with a woman as fascinating, as rare, as Camilla. A woman who was a link between a venerated tradition and the modern world.

Wouldn't any spiritual person be intrigued by such a story? Wouldn't a woman who dedicated her life to her god feel some connection to a woman who dedicated her life to her goddess?

Mother Vesta

When I was growing up, my Catholic grandmother had two pictures on her bedroom wall: one was of Jesus Christ with bleeding hands and a heart wrapped in barbed wire (I didn't learn until much later that it was thorns, not barbed wire) and the other was of Mother Mary, holding open her robe to show a flame burning in her heart.

As far as I know, these pictures had been in the same spot on the same wall for the entirety of her fifty-year marriage to my grandfather, an outspoken atheist.

Who knows what kind of discussions took place privately about this décor. I am sure my grandpa would have objected to them on principle; however, their placement on the *bedroom* wall may have been strategic on my grandma's part. Only the most short-sighted of men would start a religious argument while snuggled under the sheets with his sweetheart.

I would often sit on my grandparents' bed and chat with my grandma while she was getting ready at her dresser. Even in her later years, she had that type of movie-star glamor that the women of her generation seem to have captured the best. Since my home was nonreligious, the images on her wall held a mystical kind of allure that was largely unfamiliar to me.

The Jesus picture never did much for me – it always struck me as foreign and a bit morbid, to be honest – but I loved the picture of Mary. Her expression was motherly, warm and inviting. She had a femininity that seemed familiar and real to me. It was accessible. It reminded me of my mother and my grandmother and, as a girl, I was more drawn to that.

I think that's what I liked about Sister Maria. I would have been far more likely to strike up a friendship with a nun than a priest. I like men – I was raised by a great one, married an equally great one and am trying to raise a fantastic one – but I'm more of a woman's woman. And I guess it was that kind of feminine camaraderie that I had expected from her when I told her about Camilla.

But fundamental religious belief has a way of pre-empting one's reactions and independent thinking, and I suspect that's what happened to her when I mentioned a goddess that she had been schooled to see with contempt.

Regardless of Sister Maria's response, however, the Roman Catholic nunhood was based on the Vestal order of priestesses. The high-profile Vestal priestesses were seen daily at the Temple of Vesta, in the heart of the Roman Forum, by early Christians struggling to gain a foothold for their new cult.

The priestesses presided over many public events and there were a number of festivals dedicated to Vesta, most notably the Vestalia in June. Theirs was a tradition with a long history of public and private worship.

It was common knowledge that the Vestal priestesses were sworn to a life of celibacy during their service to the goddess, a tenet that early Catholics then adopted for their nuns. As the Vestals were married to Rome, the nuns would be married to the church and Christ. As Vestals cropped their hair and wore a headdress, so would nuns.

As the Vestals lived in the House of the Vestals, where no men were allowed to reside, nuns lived in convents. As one priestess presided over the order as the Vestalium Maxima, one nun would preside over her sisters as Mother Superior. Vestal priestesses worked alongside the Pontifix Maximus, Rome's chief pagan priest, just as Catholic nuns served under the pope who was (and still is) called the Pontifix Maximus.

Indeed, it is probable that Mary herself was based on Vesta. Like the virgin goddess Vesta – who predated Mary by more than three thousand years – the Virgin Mary's purity was held out as sacred. She was called Mother Mary, following the tradition of referring to Vesta as Mother Vesta.

It was said that Mary rode on a donkey and this animal was often associated with Mary to symbolize her modesty and poverty. Interestingly, the donkey was also the animal associated with the Temple of Vesta during its early days in Rome. The Latin poet Propertius tells us that Vesta was in those days very modest and poor, and was content with a procession of wreathed donkeys to celebrate the Vestalia.

Mary was, and continues to be, depicted with strong Vesta imagery, most notably the sacred flame that burns in her "immaculate heart." This is perhaps the most blatant symbolism taken from the Vesta tradition, and the one that resonates with me the most.

I think back to the many times I looked up at the picture of Mary on my grandmother's bedroom wall, wondering about the flame in her heart. What did it mean? Where did it come from? Now I know. The flame in Mary's heart is the sacred Flame of Vesta.

I was barely out of girlhood when I met Camilla and then Sister Maria. Now, well into middle-age, what I wouldn't do to sit down with both of them, over coffee, to talk about their two traditions and how they may have more in common than they think.

I would hope that, instead of arguing over whose is better or more truthful or more enlightened, we could come together as women, with open minds and respect, and simply enjoy each other's company.

The Sacred Feminine: A Spiritual Void

But why would the Roman Catholic church "copy" elements of the Vesta tradition? Why would they use Vestal symbolism, principles and rituals – everything from virgin purity and a celibate nunnery to the sacred flame and candle-lighting prayer – instead of creating their own religious practices from scratch?

For the same reason that I buy a package of ready-made cake mix instead of going to the grocery store, filling my cart with ingredients, and spending the day blending, kneading, folding, baking and icing. It's faster, easier, tastes as good and, in the end, very few people bother to ask if it's ready-made or made-from-scratch. In the end, everybody just wants a piece of cake.

Mary worship is a powerful tradition in the present; however, Vesta worship was an equally powerful tradition in the past. Just as devotees of Mary adore and revere their "Lady," devotees of Vesta adored and revered their goddess. And just as Catholics would fight to keep their tradition alive, so too did Vesta's faithful fight to keep her flame burning, both in their homes and in the Temple.

The Vesta tradition didn't go down quietly. It was suppressed and banished by the increasingly powerful Catholic church, and then finally criminalized upon penalty of death.

Yet Vesta's followers continued to worship and revere the goddess who had for centuries protected their families, warmed their homes, symbolized purity and perpetuity, and comforted them in times of trouble. They continued to see her face and hear her voice in the fires that heated their homes.

So when force proved ineffective, the Catholic church gave these people a new option – the cult of Mary. She was comforting, feminine, approachable and her symbolism and rituals were pacifyingly familiar. And it was a heck of a lot less risky to pray to Mary than to Vesta.

Yet there were two crucial differences between these two ladies. The first concerns their divinity: where Vesta was a powerful goddess in her own right, Mary was not a true goddess and held no independent power as a female figure. Rather, she was controlled by and subordinate to male deities, one of which was her child. This subordination was necessary to support the male-dominated doctrines of Catholicism, where men were held superior to women not only in the church, but also in society and in the home.

The second difference concerns what is called the sacred feminine: although a slippery concept to nail down, the sacred feminine can be most simply understood as spirituality that venerates the life-giving ability of women. Its spiritual principles tend to focus on themes of balance, nature, kindness, equality and harmony.

And herein lies the rub that I believe has left a spiritual void in the lives of many modern women, and men for that matter. Many people associate the modern world's male-dominated religions with themes of control, judgment, female subordination and fear. The gentler and more feminine themes of nature, harmony and equality are not fundamental precepts of today's male-dominated religions, and that doesn't sit well with a lot of people who miss the softer stuff.

Archeological evidence of the sacred feminine – that is, spirituality where goddesses held true power and women were free to openly worship female-positive themes – can be found as far back as 24, 000 BCE.

That means that for well over twenty-thousand years of the human experience, right up until the time the Vesta tradition was outlawed less than two-thousand years ago, women were free to worship in a way that spoke to them as women, wives and mothers. In way that connected them to the universe rather than subordinating them to it and to men.

There is something instinctual about the type of spirituality that the Vesta tradition embodies. It is part of who we are as women. When the Vesta tradition was banished and effectively buried, this type of spiritual expression was taken from women. I believe this has had a ripple effect of unhappiness and unfulfillment among women.

You've heard the expression "Happy wife, happy life." That's not far from the truth. When the woman in the family is unhappy, her unhappiness often has a ripple effect that can be felt throughout the home.

Her husband senses it. Her children pick up on it. The stress in the home goes up. The husband becomes distant, less affectionate or more irritable. The kids are left to walk on eggshells and may start to act out in any number of ways. I know, because I've seen it in my practice. I know, because I've lived it in my private life.

I have seen many women, professionally as clients and personally as friends or acquaintances, who have made some atrocious life-altering choices that stem from unhappiness. An extramarital affair is one of the most destructive yet common ways that a woman might try to fill a void in her life.

When a woman is trying to figure out why she feels unhappy, her marriage is usually the first thing she looks at. But she doesn't just look at it. She scrutinizes it. Analyzes it. Compares it. Criticizes it.

Minor imperfections turn into major flaws. If her husband doesn't return a text within five minutes, he is disrespecting her. If he doesn't initiate sex, he is withholding affection. If he leaves the waitress a generous tip, he is hitting on her. You get the picture.

To feel happier, a woman might sign on to social networking sites where an ex-boyfriend, old lover or new virtual friend can build her up: she's looking for a deep emotional connection, he's looking for an easy sexual one. She might start texting a male co-worker or having coffee with her personal trainer. After all, an emotional or physical affair can serve as an exhilarating distraction from a routine existence. "Maybe I'm just bored." I can't tell you how many times I've heard women say those exact words after starting a pointless affair.

But affairs aren't the only way to turn away from a husband and family – those people we love the most – in search of something to fill that void. Some women turn to anti-depressants to dull the sadness out of them. Others immerse themselves in a hobby, begin to overeat or start cracking that wine bottle open at noon. It's five o'clock somewhere, right?

Still others just give up. They succumb to their sadness and become one of the walking dead, wandering around the house with lifeless eyes and no energy, leaving their husband and children to wonder where the hell they went and if they'll ever come back.

Eat, Pray, Leave

I was several years into my couples' mediation practice when Elizabeth Gilbert's self-discovery memoir *Eat Pray Love: One Woman's Search for Everything Across Italy, India and Indonesia* became a bestseller. It was a book title that I found was being referenced by my clients on a remarkably regular basis.

The memoir is about the author who, struck by the banality of domestic life and the social expectations of women (that is, to start pumping out kids immediately after marriage), discovers that she doesn't want to be married anymore.

She walks away from her husband and keeps walking through Italy (to eat), India (to pray) and Bali (to find new love). It was the sort of book that people either loved or hated. Those who loved it saw the author as a self-aware woman who was brave enough to leave her comfort zone in search of happiness. Those who hated it saw her as a self-indulgent woman with too much money and time on her hands.

Regardless, it was one of those books that impacted some women on a personal level, especially those who wanted out of marriages not because they hated their husband, but because they didn't think they loved him as much anymore.

Why not? Because the emotional and sexual excitement of being together had worn off. Because they had drifted apart when the kids came. Because they were bored. Because they had changed. Because there had to be more to life. There was nothing wrong, it just didn't feel quite as right as they wanted it to.

I had male clients who would say, "She read a book and suddenly wanted to run off to Bali alone and find herself." Women would say, "I feel like I need to escape, to find out who I am."

I'm not blaming *Eat Pray Love* for divorce. It was the author's story to tell and people are responsible for their own choices. Plus, there are countless books in this genre, many of which resonate with their readers. Nonetheless, I found that some of my female clients, particularly those who were already unhappy or questioning their lives, were influenced by the vogue journey of self-discovery undertaken by the book's protagonist.

They identified with her and imagined themselves escaping from the banality of their family lives to exotic locales where they would taste life like never before, uncover the meaning of existence and, best of all, find a sexy soul-mate of a man who really knows how to make love. And order Chianti in Italian. I'm getting warm just thinking about that.

I know first-hand that emotions can be contagious. I've heard countless husbands complain that their wives have turned bitter or critical or negative because they have been spending a lot of time around a "man-hating" friend going through a nasty divorce.

Of course, it works the other way, too. Husbands can be influenced by a playboy buddy or a friend whose wife just left him for her "loaded" boss. It is possible to "catch" an emotion someone else is feeling.

The same kind of condition can spread through books and movies. Exotic voyages of self-discovery can lead women who are already wondering "What's it all about? Is this all life has to offer?" to voyeuristically wander down cobblestone streets and climb mountains in faraway lands, and then sit cross-legged and wide-eyed in front of an all-knowing guru or Yoda (or at least someone in a tunic who can nod in that all-knowing way) who can reveal to them the meaning of life and the path to true happiness.

Well, I know that I'd rather take that trip than fold another load of laundry. It is true that amazing things happen when we leave familiar ground and stretch our wings in skies not yet seen. That's how I met Camilla.

But the grunt work – the soul-searching, finding meaning and happiness, becoming a more spiritual person – doesn't happen on vacation in Italy, at least it didn't for me. For me, life is a journey that goes on even when the scenery is less than thrilling.

It's easy to feel awed by life and the universe when you're standing in an awe-inspiring place like the Roman Forum with wings on your feet.

It's trickier when those wings are tucked in and your kid with the stomach flu is vomiting his soup on your sheep slippers. It's trickier when work and dishes are piling up. It's trickier when your husband's socks are in the middle of the bedroom floor even though you've asked him about a gazillion times to put them in the clothes hamper.

The routine, tedious predictability of everyday life is usually seen as an obstacle to enlightenment and happiness. It's one reason we go for the "big change." Who hasn't tried for a fresh start by moving to different city, buying a new house or going on a life-changing, soul-searching vacation? And who hasn't realized that, inch by inch, the tedious predictability of life always comes creeping back.

That's why the little things are so important. You don't always need to throw away the desk you're sitting behind. Sometimes you just need to stand on top of it and take a good look around.

Finding Happiness at Home

All of which leads me to remember a conversation I once had with Sister Maria. She worked with the sick and dying, and I recall asking her what people talk about on their deathbeds. It's a morbid question, I know, but I was curious.

She told me that people talk about home and family. Almost without exception, they talk about their spouses, their children and their own parents who have already been dead for decades. They talk about the little things.

Summers at the lake cottage, family board-game nights, road trips and a child's favorite food. The first time they took the training wheels off their daughter's bicycle or how their son used to sing in the bathtub as a little boy. How he scored the game-winning shot when he was twelve or how their daughter graduated at the top of her medical school class. How their grand-daughter had the same eyes as the great-grandmother she never knew.

How their wife once caught a twenty-pound rainbow trout, but felt so sorry for it that she threw it back in the lake. How their husband used to leave a trail of socks in every single room, like Hansel and Gretel left breadcrumbs in the woods. The first words their son ever said, when his first hamster died or the first time he ever drove away in a car by himself.

They talk about happy memories, but they talk about regrets, too. How they used to yell or swear at their wife or how they were estranged from their children. How they cheated on their husband and never told him.

How they wasted so much time being angry about nothing and making problems where there weren't any and what they wouldn't do to have five minutes of that wasted time back right now, to do what they should have done, which is hug their wife or husband or kids as tightly as possible because, like it or not, we are all slowly slipping away from each other.

Which makes me wonder if we shouldn't start thinking backwards. Perhaps, just for a moment every day, we should pictures ourselves on our deathbed and imagine what memories, what people, we would want to remember and talk about.

And then we can light a candle and look into the Flame of Vesta as a reminder that our family – past, present and even future – is the surest path to happiness, meaning and sacredness in life.

I don't think that we find ourselves, or find happiness, in solitude. There is much to be said for quiet reflection; however, there is more to be said for the laughter of those we love, for the clinking of glasses at a celebration, for the barking of a family dog outside, for the slamming of doors as our kids race out to play with friends, for a husband's awful singing in the shower, for the pop of the popcorn maker to feed yet another simple but sacred family movie night.

In fact, I don't think we find ourselves at all. I think we create ourselves. And we do that when we create the microcosm that becomes our family, the circle of those we love, and when that becomes part of the universe itself. We create our own happiness, although sometimes it takes a while for us to realize it.

Self-Creation

I realized the power of self-creation when Don and I stumbled upon a tiny lookalike Temple of Vesta in Las Vegas.

I had been basting in my own unhappiness for longer than I care to admit, but the sight of the little white temple felt like a tough, no-nonsense grandmother slapping me across the face and telling me to stop self-creating unhappiness and to start self-creating happiness instead. I realized what made me happy. I realized something else, too. Something terrifying. The thing that makes me happiest in this life almost didn't happen.

My son spent the first two months of his shaky life in the Neonatal Intensive Care Unit in the Royal Alexandra Stollery Children's Hospital in Edmonton, Alberta. The medical and nursing staff there saved my son's life, and likely mine, too. Back in 2002, the hospital let moms of preemies live on-site in what used to be a nurse's residence, and I lived in a dormitory room there for the two months of his stay.

I spent my days and nights in the NICU sitting by my son's incubator. He needed to be flipped from one side to another so that his still soft cranium would form into a nice round head. He needed his tiny, doll-sized diaper changed. He needed a sponge bath. He needed the mucus pulled out of his nose with tweezers so the nasal prongs could pump oxygen into his lungs. He needed the excessive air he swallowed because of the oxygen carefully drawn out of his stomach with a syringe.

He needed someone to sit and stare at him for hours, promising him that someday soon we could take the intravenous needle out of his head and take him home.

Late one evening, when the hospital was quiet and visitors were long gone, I went into a supply room to get some glass bottles in which to store my breast milk. As I was collecting them, a nurse with whom I had become friends came in to grab some supplies she needed.

As we chatted, I happened to notice a beautiful white bassinet tucked into the corner. I hadn't seen it before and in a world of medical glass incubators, it was out of place.

"That's pretty," I said.

"We use it when we take pictures of the dead babies," she said. "To give to the parents."

I think about that sometimes. Had my son not made it, I honestly don't know if Don and I would have made it either. The grief might have been too heavy to carry. I think about how close I came to not having the life I have. Had our son not made it, would I have retreated into my career and walked away from Don and the pain? Probably.

When you spend a lot of time in the hospital, you see parts of the human experience that are inherently private and breathtakingly poignant. They give you perspective. They make you very aware that life is a story, but birth and death are the bookends. That's not necessarily a bad thing. If we didn't know the story had to end, we wouldn't bother telling it well.

> All beauteous things for which we live
> By laws of time and space decay.
> But O, the very reason why
> I clasp them, is because they die.
> - William Johnson Cory, *Mimnermus in Church*

Hospitals are different at night than they are during the day. They're quieter, more informal, almost like a massive institutionalized bedroom. Not all departments, of course: the emergency department, the operating room, the labs, these probably aren't a lot different. But the patient floors are.

I know this, because the nurses' residence in which I stayed was at the opposite end of the hospital as the NICU, and I'd make the trek a few times each night, often in the middle of the night.

At those hours, only the hard-core visitors are left. A mom and dad holding a kidney basin for their cancer-stricken five-year-old to vomit into. Or wiping a feverish child's forehead with a cool cloth. Or agonizing over whether to unplug the life support system that a drunk driver hooked their sixteen-year-old daughter up to.

At the Royal Alex, there was a long glass corridor, a walkway, that joined the original hospital building to the larger, modern complex. When you walked through the corridor, you could see through what used to be the outside windows of the hospital building, directly into patient rooms. The corridor was up high, perhaps half way up the building, and far below there was a seating area, a little coffee bar and a piano.

I liked walking through this corridor. You could hear voices and sounds echoing and it was kind of cool, especially at night.

I was making a late-night trek through this walkway when I heard someone playing the piano far below. The music was resonating up into the space between the two buildings, between the stone façade of the original hospital building and the glass of the new complex. The song was lovely but melancholy.

As the music softly reverberated into my space, I looked across the void between the two buildings, through a window and into a patient room.

There was an old man on a hospital bed, the head of the bed elevated so that he could sit up. His wife was sitting beside him. They were holding hands and talking. I remember wondering what they were talking about, and whether they were enjoying the music.

I felt like I was in the middle of an impromptu, nostalgic music video. Like that Leonard Cohen masterpiece, *Dance Me to the End of Love*, where he sings in that god-like, ageless voice as old married couples waltz in front of giant black-and-white pictures of them when they were a young couple and, every once in a while, one of them sits alone on a chair and looks at their wedding picture, staring into the youthful eyes of the bride or groom who has gone before them.

As you climb into your bed tonight, all these things will be happening at a hospital near you. And if you haven't yet seen such things in your life, fear not. You will, and not always as a spectator.

I don't need to escape to Bali to find myself or climb a mountain to achieve enlightenment through a guru. I know as much about life as anyone else, no matter how flowing their robe or exotic their accent.

And what I've learned about my life is that love and spirituality don't need to be uprooted or transplanted to thrive. They grow where we plant them. They give us roots that let us reach higher than any mountain top.

CHAPTER VII

Finding a Focal Point

The intuitive mind is a sacred gift.
  - Albert Einstein

How ridiculous, and what a stranger he is, to be surprised at anything that happens in life.
  - Marcus Aurelius, Emperor of Rome, 121 – 180 CE

It wasn't divine intervention that brought me to the Temple of Vesta, Las Vegas style, in November of 2012, over twenty years after I'd visited the real temple in Rome. It wasn't divine inspiration that made me look at it and see my life. It was a choice. A choice to find meaning in the moment and to make it last. A subconscious choice, perhaps, but a choice all the same.

After that experience, I chose to act differently. I chose to find Camilla's candle and show it the respect and reverence it deserved. I chose to show my family the same things. They didn't know about the choice, but they did know there was a change.

The month after I excavated Camilla's candle from my mom's basement, in the deep freeze of mid-December, Don sprung a "snow celebration" weekend on me. This was around the same time – December 2012 – that the world was supposed to end, at least according to some wonky interpretation of the Mayan calendar.

We went tobogganing, took a winter night drive into the country, came home to ice wine and cold cuts and curled up in front of the fireplace to watch John Carpenter's horror classic *The Thing,* which is set in the frozen wastes of the Antarctic. And which is probably the only Hollywood movie I've ever seen that realistically portrays c-c-c-cold.

Typically, something called a "snow celebration" would have boiled my blood and set me off on a temper tantrum. "You want to celebrate snow? You know I hate snow!" But I made a choice to celebrate what he was doing for me. To celebrate *him.* And in the process, I realized that much of our happiness – and unhappiness – is self-chosen.

Did you ever hear that old legend about the two wolves? It goes like this. One evening, an old Cherokee grandfather was talking to his grandson about a battle that goes on inside every person, every day.

He said, "The battle is between two wolves. One wolf is anger, jealousy, regret, hatred, unhappiness, resentment, ego, self-pity and self-doubt. The other wolf is serenity, gratitude, perspective, love, joy, empathy, humor, kindness and conviction."

The grandson asks, "Which wolf will win the battle?"

And the grandfather answers, "The one you feed."

The Power of Focus

It took me years to realize that I had a spiritual void in my life and to understand how faith could fill that void.

I now live a much brighter life by choosing to focus on the things that make me happy, that I feel are divine and that give me a sense of reassurance that "the universe is unfolding as it should." (Max Ehrmann, *Desiderata*)

There are many people like me: people who reject strict religious doctrine and supernatural beliefs, but who nonetheless long for a type of spiritual expression. Who feel an instinctual awe when they look up at the stars or look into a flame.

To me, Vesta is an anthropomorphized representation of the very essence of life, a beautiful flame and face that makes the immensity of the universe just a little more intimate.

Her flame is also a lighthouse for those lost in a sea of unhappiness or troubles. It is a beautiful light to focus on as one rows to shore. So much of this faith is – and always has been – about focus. Focusing on the positive, not the negative. On hope, not despair. On moving forward, not sticking in the past. On what we want to happen to us, not what has happened to us. On what we have, not what we think we need.

For too long, I didn't do this in my own life. I didn't take the time to get my life into focus before steamrolling ahead. No wonder I crashed into so many things along the way.

I did the same steamrolling in my practice, too. When a woman would talk about how unhappy she was in her life and relationship, I would equip her with better communication skills, problem-solving strategies, and ideas to improve intimacy and interactions. These were all good things but, too often, I didn't start at the beginning. I didn't encourage her to put her life as an individual into focus first. I didn't help her get inspired and therefore she didn't have enough positive energy to do the grunt work it sometimes takes to save a marriage.

What we focus on gets clearer and brighter. Focusing on the flame of faith and everything it represents can ensure that happiness fills the frame. It can give us the spiritual focus, the positive feelings and outlook, that we need to make good things happen in our lives.

Staying Focused

Unfortunately, I'd always found it easier to get focused than to stay focused. If I wanted to organize my office, I'd buy a small fortune's worth of office supplies, but I'd lose steam before I actually got around to packing away those old files.

If I wanted to eat healthier, I'd come home from the grocery store with bags of organic produce, but I'd lose momentum before I got around to washing it and instead it would all rot, forgotten and uneaten, on the bottom shelf of the fridge. I had the noblest of intentions, but my follow-through was pathetic.

I didn't want that to happen with Vesta. Her tradition had made life better and brighter for my whole family, and I didn't want to lose that ground. I knew it all hinged on me. I knew that if I started to backslide in my newfound spirituality, if I started to break the new habits I had adopted or let my emotions run rampant like they used to, I'd fall back into my old ways and lose all the progress I'd made. Everything was going so well. I didn't want to screw it up.

The presence of the lararium and my small, everyday efforts at defamiliarization went a long way to helping me stay on-track; however, I began to long for a more personal way to stay focused. Something more internal, something more…I don't know, *spiritual*.

I knew that I felt most focused when burning a Vestal candle, so I started burning one at my desk at work; however, I was so preoccupied at work that more than once I left the office without extinguishing it. I needed a better ritual, one with more practicality and less liability.

Years ago, I had a friend who used to meditate whenever and wherever he felt stressed or out of sorts. And when I say *whenever and wherever* he felt these things, that's exactly what I mean. It didn't matter if he were on the train, writing an exam, at a rock concert or walking through a drug store.

If he felt like something had "rattled his Zen" he'd stop in his tracks, pinch his fingers together, close his eyes and regain his mindfulness and self-control. He was like a spiritual narcoleptic, falling into spontaneous trances without warning. But he was also the most focused person I've ever known: one of those annoying yet admirable people who actually manage to finish what they start.

So I decided to combine his way of staying focused with my own. Instead of just letting a Vestal candle burn for hours beside me as I worked on the computer or made supper, hoping I would somehow subconsciously absorb some focus from the flame, I decided I'd take a more structured approach.

One morning after Don had left for work and our son was munching his breakfast cereal at the table, I decided to practice a few minutes of light meditation. So to speak.

"I'm going into my bedroom for a few minutes," I told my son. "Don't bother me unless it's an emergency, okay?"

"Okay, mom." He didn't take his eyes off the back of the cereal box.

"Promise?"

No measurable response. Just loud chewing and a hint of a head nod.

I went into my bedroom and closed the door behind me. I sat cross-legged on the bed, lit a Vestal candle on my nightstand, and took a deep, relaxing, focusing breath. I didn't do anything fancy. None of the meditative breath exercises my friend used to try to teach me. I just focused on how the breath felt moving in and out of my lungs, and how my muscles and then my mind seemed to unwind until they felt strangely weightless.

The flickering flame looked radiant in my still dimly-lit bedroom, and its crackle sounded amazing in the early morning silence of my house. I focused on it. My emotions seemed to settle into a state of calm and my thoughts naturally gravitated toward how good things had become. Toward feelings of affection for my husband and son.

And then, out of the corner of my eye, I noticed movement. A piece of paper slid under the bedroom door. Upon it, in heavy black marker, was written, "Mom, I can't find any clean socks. It's an emergency. Please help."

Yet even the precious few minutes I had spent in reflection – focusing my thoughts and emotions and feeling positive about my life – had been enough to set the tone for the rest of the day.

It gave me the spark I needed to reflect not just upon my faith, but also upon my family and the type of person I wanted to be for them. It gave me an edge. Instead of being irritated by my son's interruption, I couldn't help but laugh at it. A good thought had sparked a good thing.

A Face in the Flame

Over the next weeks, I refined and expanded this "light reflection" practice until I found a way to incorporate it into my daily life without notes being slid under the door, my smart phone beeping, the doorbell ringing or the dog barking.

I discovered that it gave me precisely the kind of simple staying-power that I needed to stay committed to my newfound faith. The sparks of good thoughts and emotions that happened during these times of light reflection served the same purpose as the daily affirmations or devotionals practiced in other faiths.

At first, it felt ridiculous. Forced and artificial. Me – high-strung, impatient, restless – trying to act like some kind of meditating yogi. Although there was nobody else in the room, I felt embarrassed anyway. But as I looked into the flame, as I heard it crackle, the self-consciousness melted away to reveal something else underneath. A face.

The New Vesta tradition had become part of our daily life. We burned a Vestal candle during meals and sprinkled olive oil into the flame as an offering. It had become an important household ritual. The lararium was a physical reminder of family unity and history.

This Vestal spirituality had given me perspective and patience and made our home a happier place. It had made me feel reverence for my life and my family.

But had I really felt reverence for Vesta herself? I was like an actor who had devoutly performed *Hamlet,* who knew every word, scene and nuance of the play and who revered the lines as divine poetry that spoke the very meaning of life – but who hadn't yet connected with the playwright. Shakespeare. The one who made it all happen.

I loved the Vesta tradition. But it took a while to love Vesta, too, and to realize that her spirit was distinct from the spirituality of her principles and practices. That her face was in the flame and that she had a personality. I started to feel her presence in my life as a friend and guide, instead of just a set of ideas and rituals. She was more than her history. She had to be: otherwise, how could she exist in the present? In the future?

For the first time in my life, I started to do something that was completely and utterly out of character for me, something that I swore I would never do, something that was totally unrecognizable to my former self: I started to pray. I actually got down onto my knees, before the Vestal candle and the statue of Vesta on my lararium, and prayed to her.

Actually, "prayed" is the wrong word. I didn't ask for anything. I just talked to her. About stuff. Sometimes it was important stuff, like the fact that my parents were getting older and I was getting worried about them, or that I had taken on too many clients and wasn't spending as much time with my family as I should've been. Other times it was trivial. Should I change my hair color? Should we let our son get a pet snake?

Sometimes a loud crackle would pop out of the flame and I'd take it as an answer. Other times, I'd simply look into the flame and see the answer reflected back as in a mirror, while a trail of willowy vapor burned off the wooden wick and floated up to the ceiling.

Women's Intuition

I was admiring the pretty, wispy convolutions of the flame's vapor one afternoon when a thought formed in my mind. This thought formed in the same way that, if you look long enough at the clouds, you will eventually see a shape take form – an elegant swan, a tall ship, a bare-chested gladiator. Okay, that last one is a bit salty, but you get the idea.

The thought went something like this:

Don took his trike to work this morning. I hate that trike. I don't trust it. It's too old. It's just a matter of time until it breaks down and leaves him stranded, or worse. In fact, I can almost picture him on the side of the road right now. But it's the middle of the afternoon, so that's impossible. He's at his desk, at work. Unless he's having an affair on me...then he wouldn't be at work. Man, I hate how paranoid I get when I have PMS. Still, something doesn't feel right. I'm going to call him.

I got up and dialed his work number. No answer. I dialed his cell number. This time, he answered – but his voice was heavy and labored. Like he was out of breath. Like he'd just rolled off his twenty-something cheerleader lover and was drained from sexual exertion.

"Where are you?" I asked.

"I'm...I'm..."

"Where?"

"I'm broken down on the side of the road," he said. "The engine in my trike blew."

"Why aren't you at work?"

"I was at work," he sighed heavily, "but there's a big storm moving in, so I wanted to get the trike home before it hits."

"Oh."

"I need you to hook up the trailer to the car and come get me."

It was a stressful drive to rescue him – I hate pulling a trailer behind the car – but it was also a trip full of revelation as I replayed Camilla's words in my mind.

"*L'intuizione delle donne*...when a woman has focus, she can see more."

It wasn't PMS paranoia that had put me on alert. It was women's intuition. I was tapping into abilities I hadn't before noticed or used. Perhaps there was something to this "prayer thing" after all.

There's a popular idea that we as humans only use about ten percent of our brain. It may have been the early 20th century book *The Energies of Men*, written by a psychologist named William James, that introduced this provocative idea to us. In it, he claims that people make use of only a small part of their potential mental and physical resources. Wow. Can you imagine what feats we'd be capable of if only we could tap into that other ninety percent?

Of course, this isn't strictly the case. Brain imaging scans have shown that we do use all of our brain for even the simplest of tasks like walking or eating. Yet I wholeheartedly agree that most of us don't use all of the mental and physical resources available to us as human beings. Most of us never live up to our full potential.

But that's not always a tragic thing. I didn't live up to my full potential to be a high-powered, pencil-skirt wearing lawyer. I did, however, tap into other potential – spiritual potential – and the power to create a life that I loved.

The word "potential" implies an ability to develop something in the future, particularly something "potent." As I focused on Vesta's flame – on that energy that had burned for millennia – I realized that it was showing me something powerful about my own abilities. It was showing me the power of a woman's intuition.

Women's intuition – a female sixth sense – is something that most women are familiar with, at least in theory. In practice, however, we don't always tap into it. There have been many times in my life that I've ignored it, and always to my own detriment.

So I made a conscious choice to start tuning in to it, especially during those times I was in light reflection or prayer (for lack of a better word).

I would focus on an important question – Should I let our son start walking to school by himself? Am I feeling healthy? Is my marriage strong? – and then I would wait quietly and let my mind, spirit and body answer it. I would work out the question by instinct.

I discovered that it is possible to "intuit" an answer to certain questions. As I knelt in front of Vesta's flame and felt the warmth radiate onto my face, I also felt my emotions exploring the questions. I felt my gut instinct kick-in. And that's where I would find the answers. By the light of the flame, by the twinge of my gut.

No, he isn't old enough to walk to school alone. No, I've been too sluggish; I need to start exercising more. Yes, my marriage is strong, but Don and I haven't had a romantic getaway in months, and it's long overdue. Buy something sexy and book a room.

The truth is, gut instinct – especially the kind we tap into during times of reflection or prayer – can give us the clarity to answer important questions. It plays a big part in intuition. There are neurotransmitters in our gut that, not unlike the neurotransmitters in our brain, respond to the stimuli of emotion (fear, love, worry) and environmental factors (a dark back alley).

Yet women's intuition is more ethereal, more elegant than just neurotransmitters and stimuli. It's the sort of thing that is best seen by sacred candlelight. I know for a fact that focusing on Vesta's flame has done precisely what Camilla told me it would do. It helped me see and feel things more clearly. I saw things I could only have seen by Vesta's light.

I could anticipate things better, too. It was as though I knew when Don was going to come home in a bad mood or our son was going to come home from school feeling melancholy or upset. I knew it was going to happen before it happened, and I knew what to do about it. My woman's intuition helped me connect to the people I loved in a higher, almost inexplicable way.

In ancient times – long before we had smoke alarms, cell phones or social media alerts – I suspect that women were far more tuned-in to their intuition. We've all heard stories along the lines of a sleeping mother who, sensing something is wrong with her child, wakes up and goes to his room. She puts her hand on his forehead as he sleeps, only to discover that he has a raging fever. It was this type of ability that I felt I was once again tuning-in to.

This intuition wasn't just focused on my family, though. I soon discovered that, as I looked into the flame, I was able self-intuit as well. That is, I was more perceptive of my own needs, whether they were to retreat for a quiet night or lose myself in a good belly-laugh. Self-intuition, as flighty as that still sounds to me, is now an important part of my spirituality and overall well-being.

Prayer was something that I had always considered to be the most concocted and useless thing a person could waste her time doing; however, it turned out to be one of the most natural and useful things I'd ever done.

I found that faith had an amazing, real-world purpose. Praying to Vesta, focusing on her sacred flame, had illuminated part of my being that I wouldn't have otherwise seen – my woman's and self-intuition. And that, quite frankly, surprised the hell out of me.

CHAPTER VIII

Vesta, Renewed

So long as a person is capable of self-renewal, they are a living being.
- Henri Frederick Amiel, Swiss Philosopher, 1821 – 1881 CE

Somewhere to the eastward a wolf howled; lightly, questioningly. I knew the voice, for I had heard it many times before.
- Farley Mowat, *Never Cry Wolf.* Canadian Author, 1921 – 2014 CE

New Beginnings

From adult baptisms to renewing your marriage vows, people are drawn to the idea of a new beginning, a fresh start. I'm no exception.

For most of my life, I've had this weird idea in my head that if I woke up at 3:15 am, I could start my life over again. That all my past mistakes would stay in the past and I could move forward in a new, better, happier way.

I used to think there was something auspicious about that time. That maybe the 3:15 am idea was planted in my mind by the universe and had some kind of supernatural ability to give me a fresh start; however, I've since learned that 3:15 am is the time in the *Amityville Horror* movie when the protagonist would wake up to horrors happening in the haunted house.

Reality check. My 3:15 am idea wasn't given to me by the universe, it was given to me by Hollywood. It was probably planted in my brain at ten years old when I accidentally saw the movie commercial on TV and had terror struck into my little kid heart. I'll bet I spent a month sleeping in my parents' bed.

In any event, it does go to show that most of us love the idea of a do-over. The idea that we can in some way renew our life or our being. I was so drawn to it that my mind constructed my own fresh start out of a horror flick.

Fire Power: Cleansing and Renewing

Symbolic cleansing and renewal rituals are seen in almost all cultures and religions. The Vesta tradition of renewing the Flamma Vesta once a year was, and still is, a very important ritual.

In antiquity, this happened on the first day of March, the first day of the Roman calendar. Then as now, New Year's Day is the ultimate new beginning. It's full of promise and hope, and personal resolutions to do things differently, better, from now on, without looking back.

The living Flame of Vesta is itself a cleansing and renewing element. It purifies whatever it engulfs, and produces pure potential from the ashes. Fire has that quality to it.

I remember driving through Canada's Yoho National Park a few years after a major forest fire had swept through it. All along the mountainsides there were large patches of grey, burned, brittle trees that stretched on for miles and miles, like so many ash-colored spikes sticking out of the ground.

Yet at the base of these dead trees was the most vibrant green growth I've ever seen. Life was coming back.

A forest fire consumes everything in its path; however, it also encourages new, healthy forest growth. It promotes rebirth. It cleanses an old forest of its dominant species of vegetation, the one that may be preventing a variety of new life from flourishing, and it rids the trees and forest floor of bugs that spread disease and death.

Indeed, some species of trees can only grow after a fire. The Jack Pine, for example, needs fire to survive and thrive. Older trees are often seen with brown, dead branches that remain on the tree for years, ruining the resplendent green of the healthier foliage. When the tree feels the heat of fire, its cones open to release their seeds. The seeds germinate on the purified ground and a new tree springs from the seed and spirit of the old one.

Once a forest fire cleanses the ground and burns away many years of dead foliage and rotting wood, the diversity and abundance of life that had been waiting dormant under its weight, trapped in the dark, can once again feel the warmth of the sun and experience life anew. The seeds of flowers and berries that had been dormant for decades can germinate into colorful life.

Yet it is a painful experience. It is heart wrenching to see trees that have stood for so long burn away and fall to ash. It's terrifying. It's hard to accept it and let it happen. We have been conditioned to reach for a bucket of water to try and stop it. Even when it's all for the greater good, it can be an excruciating experience.

The same goes with life and letting go of our past. Our past mistakes, disappointments, losses, betrayals or heartaches. They are brown branches on what could be, should be, a vibrant green tree, but they've been there for so long that we can't imagine what we'd look like, feel like, without them. Only something as strong and as sacred as fire can burn them away and give us that fresh start. That new growth. Even when it hurts, we have to let it happen.

Even Vesta has had to let go of her past and embrace a new future.

Letting go of our past expectations is a similar process. I had all kinds of expectations about my life. High-powered law career, jet-setting lifestyle and an urbane, child-free existence.

None of those expectations came to pass and it wasn't always an easy or painless process to let them go. I spent a lot of time looking back before I was able to look ahead. Yet now I cannot believe that I ever wanted a different way of life. What a fool I was.

If we are to grow, we may also need to let go of long-held personal belief – or in my case non-belief – so that we can renew our lives and the way we look at the world. As a non-religious person who began to embrace spirituality, I often felt that part of my former self was being burned away. It was at times a painful, humbling and uniquely vulnerable experience.

I remember one dark night in particular that I was really struggling with the process. I kept vacillating between my entrenched atheism and emerging Vestal beliefs, my skeptical side at war with my spiritual side.

It was only then that I realized that belief, like happiness, is also a choice. It was up to me whether I chose to back-track and return to my previous worldview – faithless, cynical, sometimes even surly – or whether I wanted to keep exploring this new path, the path lit by Vesta.

I thought a lot that night about the Cherokee story of the two wolves. The wolf was a prominent and esteemed symbol of vitality and honor in ancient Rome.

Romulus, the legendary founder of Rome – and son of the first Vestal priestess Rhea Silvia – was suckled by a she-wolf after he was left to die in the forest by his mother's enemy. Romans didn't fear the "big bad wolf." They revered the wolf as a representation of personal strength and survival.

As the Flamma Vesta crackled before me, I closed my eyes and pictured myself in a forest on fire. I could feel the heat and smell the smoke.

I heard a crackle in front of me. Not the crackle of the flame, but the crackle of branches as the wolves, one white and one black, walked over the smoldering, snapping tree roots to approach me.

I thought about what each wolf represented. The black wolf was darkness, disappointment and disillusionment. It was always hungry, never happy. It was eager and sharp, but also restless.

The white wolf was light, love and gratitude. It felt happiness, not hunger. And while it was as eager and sharp as its companion, it was also at peace with its life. To me, the white wolf represented Vesta and the profound changes she had brought to my life, marriage and family.

I imagined myself kneeling down and extending my hand to the white wolf. I visualized it walking toward me and pressing its cool, white muzzle into my palm, perhaps eating some unseen food from my hand.

To me, it was an act of cleansing my former self and purifying my past. It was an act of making a choice and renewing my worldview in a way that reflected the woman I had become in the two decades since I had first received the Flamma Vesta.

Yet it was a choice that I couldn't have seen coming. To choose the very things that I had rejected and ridiculed for most of my life – faith, spirituality, family life, peace, gratitude – was a humbling experience. But it was also an enlightening one. As much as I value remaining true to one's beliefs, I also value having an open-mind and an open-heart so that those beliefs have the ability to change, if change is what's needed. I certainly needed it.

If life can be reborn from lifelessness, just as new growth can spring from the charred Earth, shouldn't our beliefs about that life be as adaptive and tenacious? To me, that kind of adaptivity and tenaciousness is the very spirit of life and renewal.

CHAPTER IX

Liturgy and the Light of Vesta

It seemed to be a necessary ritual that he should prepare himself for sleep by meditating under the solemnity of the night sky...a mysterious transaction between the infinity of the soul and the infinity of the universe.
- Victor Hugo, French Novelist, 1802 – 1885 CE

To love rightly is to love what is orderly and beautiful in an educated and disciplined way.
- Plato, Greek Philosopher, 4th Century BCE

    Just as I was thinking about an ending for this book, an ending happened. My best friend's dad, whom I'd known for most of my life, died. Theirs is a close family and his death hit them hard.

    My last memory of him was the previous summer, when Don, our son and I had visited him in Vancouver. He brought us wild berries and ice cream in his backyard and then showed off his garden of vine-ripened tomatoes.

He was Greek, and his thick accent and Old World eyes reminded me a bit of Camilla. Like her, he had a quick wit and an even quicker smile. Like her, his face told a story and his nature drew people in.

Greek Tragedy

When I say that my best friend's family is Greek, I mean that they are *really* Greek. They speak in Greek, think in Greek, cook in Greek, read Greek newspapers, watch Greek soap operas and call me by my Greek name of Despina. My friend, Alyssa, went to Greek school.

Other than some professors and school-mates, she's the only person I've ever known who can talk easily to me about the Greco-Roman gods and goddesses, including Vesta, and who seems to feel their presence in the world. Theirs is a family and culture steeped in a long, rich tradition.

I remember many years ago when Alyssa's sister moved out of the family home. It was scandalous for unwed Greek girls to move out of their parents' house before marriage and, since her parents had company on the day of the move, she was forced to surreptitiously move her belongings – including her bed – out of her second-storey bedroom window so as not to alarm the guests that were enjoying Greek coffee and baklava downstairs in the living room.

With the mattress hanging half-in and half-out the high window, perilously dangling above the lawn outside, her mother cracked open the bedroom door and peeked into the room. "Be quiet," she said in Greek, "the company will hear!"

Such Greek goings-on were what I loved about my friend's family. Never a dull moment.

As Don and I packed to leave for Vancouver and the funeral, Alyssa called me to explain that her father's funeral and burial were to be in the strict Greek Orthodox tradition.

"You know those types of funerals that celebrate a life?" she asked me. "The kind that try to be joyful?"

"Yes," I said.

"Well, this won't be one of them," she sighed. "We're the culture that created the Greek tragedy, don't forget."

Alpha and Omega

And so a few days later I found myself back where my love of religious architecture and ritual began – in an Orthodox Catholic church. In my childhood, it was the modest St. George's in blue-collar Flin Flon, Manitoba. Now, it was the much grander St. Nicholas's in urban Vancouver, British Columbia.

It had taken four decades to connect the two dots, but the moment I saw the dome of St. Nicholas break the skyline the timeline between the two points closed in as if not a day had gone by.

As a kid, I used to sit on the church steps and stare up at the cupola, or dome, of St. George's. A soaring symbol of heaven, this architectural feature tops the roofs of all Orthodox churches and gives them their distinct look and feel. Of course, the dome atop St. Nicholas was more impressive than St. George's; however, I felt a pang of nostalgia for my little street-corner church just the same.

I felt nostalgic for the Temple of Vesta, too, that ancient dome-topped temple whose ruins I had first stumbled upon so long ago and whose round cupola similarly represented the infinite universe and the circle of life.

It struck me how life ultimately takes us in these kinds of circles, despite the perception that we're moving straight ahead, through the years and events, through friendships and joys and sorrows, in some kind of illusionary linear march through time.

It's the whole Biblical "ashes to ashes" thing. A beginning and an end, Alpha and Omega. Existence buttressed by non-existence at each end, or more poetically, a dream rounded with a sleep, as Shakespeare so eloquently said.

One way or another, we all end up where we started.

Ritual and Doctrine

As long as I can remember, I've been in love with ritual. To this day, when I open a box of Smarties, I pour them all onto the table and eat the red ones last. I love religious ritual, too. For me, the problem has been that ritual and doctrine – the latter being rules that dictate what you must believe or how you must behave – are usually a two-for-one-deal. And I've never been too crazy about being told what to think or do.

On those long ago Sunday mornings that I'd accompany Sister Maria to Roman Catholic Mass, I'd remain seated in the wooden pew as a procession of faithful strolled by me to the front of the church to receive Communion.

Oh, how I longed to tag along and give it a shot. What did those little round wafers taste like? (I had no idea at that time that the wafers used in Catholic Mass were based on the mola salsa wafers the Vestals prepared and offered to the goddess.) Was the wine (a practice also taken from Vestal libation to the goddess) any good? Would the spiritual solemnity of the ritual change my life?

But alas, it was not to be. As Sister Maria told me, I didn't meet any of the doctrinal requirements the Catholic church lays out for those who wish to receive Communion. I hadn't been baptized or attended confession, I didn't believe in transubstantiation (the idea that the bread and wine become the actual living body and blood of Christ) and I didn't observe the Eucharist fast. I have a hard time making it from breakfast to lunch without a meal to tide me over.

Yet according to the church, I did – and still do, in case you're wondering – meet the requirements for being in a "state of grace." I've never murdered anyone, had an abortion, participated in a homosexual act, had extramarital or premarital sex or engaged in an impure thought…oh wait, that last one is a stickler. Guilty as charged. It's hard not have the occasional impure thought when you've watched as many gladiator movies as I have.

Other than murder – I'm with the Pope on giving that a big no-no – I disagree with much Catholic doctrine. I support a woman's right to make her own reproductive choices, and I'm behind same-sex marriage all the way. I couldn't care less if people engage in premarital sex. That's their business. And a few impure thoughts can add a spark to a dreary workday, can't they?

Which all brings me back to where I've always been: longing for the ritual, but unable to participate because I can't get on board with doctrine.

In any event, Don and I were barely through the doors of St. Nicholas Orthodox church when centuries of entrenched religious ritual hit us fast and hard. Just inside the doors, black-clad funeral attendees lit beeswax candles on a rack, thus making an offering to their god and lighting a flame for the soul of the departed.

But where others saw the light of Christ, I saw the Flame of Vesta. Candle-lighting rituals are central to the Orthodox and Catholic traditions, but these were borrowed from the candle and fire-lighting rituals that first took place in the Vestal tradition. Enlightening information, to be sure, but not the type of lesson one preaches to funeral attendees in the antechamber of an Orthodox church. It's just bad form.

Perched near the candle rack was what the Greek Orthodox church calls the Holy Theotokas, a picture – an icon, really – of the Virgin Mary. After lighting a candle, funeral attendees either kissed this icon or made the sign of the cross in front of it.

Again, where others saw the face of Mary, I saw the face of her predecessor, Vesta. I could almost hear Sister Maria whispering in one of my ears, while Camilla whispered in the other. "Pick me!"

And then the solemn procession into the church and an elaborate funeral service, entirely in Greek, during which three chanters sang from the Bible and the presiding priest waved a thurible – a metal container hanging from a chain, within which burned incense – back and forth in front of the coffin.

The fragrant smoke rose up to the church's ceiling as an offering to their god, in the same way that it rose to the top of the temple when Vesta's faithful offered it their goddess. And it all happened in front of a white marble altar that could have been taken from the Temple of Vesta itself.

And then another procession as mourners approached the coffin in respectful order, kissing the icon that lay on top of it. Or in my non-Orthodox case, simply placing a hand of friendship and fond memories of baklava on the coffin's smooth wood.

And then finally the last procession to the cemetery for interment amid strict Greek Orthodox ceremony. A clear blue sky and vibrant green grass separated by some two-hundred mourners dressed all in black. They moved collectively as one creature, drifting and shape-shifting between the blue sky and the green grass like a giant pool of black ink.

As they lowered the coffin into the ground, I thought about the coin that Alyssa's brother had placed under the lapel of his father's jacket. It was a ritual that extended far back into Greek and Roman antiquity, thousands of years before the rise of Christianity, when family members placed a coin in the mouth or hand of their deceased loved one. The coin was to pay the ferryman Charon for passage across the River Styx, the river that separated the world of the living from the world of the dead.

Over fifteen hundred years after the banishment of the Vestal tradition and still we are performing the very same rituals that Vesta's worshippers performed. A complete circle of ritualistic practice, one that connects the past with the present and even the future. And that's what the eternal Flame of Vesta is all about.

Ritual and Realization

As I stood in the Orthodox church during the funeral service, ritual dripping from every wall and stained glass window, I realized for the first time in my life that spiritual ritual wasn't just cool, it was comforting. It wasn't just natural, it was necessary, too.

Shortly after I met Camilla in Rome in 1989, I spent a month or so in London, England, working as an office temp and living with a really fun English room-mate named Zoe. With Zoe, it was one crisis after another. Her boyfriend cheated on her. Her dog got run over. Her boss hit on her. She was groped on the Tube. She slept through her best friend's wedding. She was wrongfully arrested for shoplifting. Stuff like that.

Each time a crisis arose, Zoe did exactly the same thing. She sighed, put her hands on her hips, and said, "I'm making tea." And then she'd go through the exact same elaborate tea-making process: boiling the water, steeping the tea, wrapping the teapot in a cozy and arranging cups, saucers, biscuits, teaspoons, cream and sugar on a serving tray. "It's what we English do," she said. "Whenever there's a crisis, we make tea."

That makes sense to me now. It isn't the tea, it's the ritual. From boiling the water to filling the teacups, the entire process fills a void. A void of uncertainty, of wondering what to do in the immediate aftermath of emotional shock.

It reminds me of the sitcom *The Big Bang Theory*. Whenever the brilliant but socially-inept Sheldon finds himself in the company of a distraught friend, he falls back on the simple social grace taught to him by his mother and offers the person a hot beverage.

It's expected behavior. It's ritualistic behavior. And it helps. It gives us something to focus on, something to do with our hands, when it feels like the world is crumbling around us. During the church funeral service, I saw how those rituals comforted Alyssa and her family, and how they served as a sort of bridge between sorrow and survival. How they held them up when they just wanted to fall down.

Before coming to this realization, I had held a lot of resentment toward Christianity and the church. After all, I had learned about its history while at university and while doing my own research into the Vestal order.

I knew how the church had vandalized and violated the Vestal tradition, and how it had brutalized its faithful until they had no choice but to abandon Vesta and adopt Christ. I knew how it had taken Vesta's great traditions and rituals and claimed them as its own. And I was on a mission, a crusade of sorts, to tell the world about it.

But after the funeral service, I found that the fight had gone out of me. I looked around at the mourners, many of whom were devout Orthodox, and saw that they were good, sincere people doing their best to help a family cope with a deep loss. The priest had helped Alyssa's dad find comfort and peace at the end of his life, in great part simply by befriending him.

These were not the same people who stripped the marble off Vesta's temple, who stamped out her flame and criminalized her worship. Why should I resent them for the sins of their fathers?

I'm not naïve enough to think they would embrace my brand of spirituality or even respect it. Frankly, I don't believe they would. But I don't care. Peaceful co-existence is enough. Imagine the world we would live in if everyone lost the angry drive to "fight the good fight," and instead put down their swords and just went home. If tribes and factions and nations realized that they don't have to convert or conquer, they just have to co-exist.

I know that many people experience the kind of spiritual dilemma that I did. On one hand, they are comforted by the ritual of religion. On the other hand, they are at personal odds with aspects of its doctrines, particularly those that contradict scientific fact, violate human rights, or do not reflect progressive social values or individual morality.

Some of these people choose to remain in their religion: they just "tune out" the doctrine they don't like. Others leave the church altogether and go it alone. That was Don. Still others never get around to signing up in the first place. That was me.

More and more, we are seeing a worldwide movement away from organized religion and toward personal spirituality. This includes revisiting aspects of ancient belief systems.

In my opinion, the New Vesta tradition would do the world good. For starters, it promotes gender equality by advancing the truth that the feminine is just as divine as the masculine: as such, there is no "divine justification" for women to be seen or treated as subordinate beings to men.

Its reverence for the home can enhance a woman's family life, so that marriages and families stay intact. In the same way, it can serve strong, self-reliant men who wish to revere their families, and to love and praise their wife and children above all. If marriages are to last and families are to stay together, that shift in the male mindset will also need to be made. There are as many men as women who are open to a dynamic spirituality that reflects their values.

The New Vesta tradition can provide a spiritual focus for the entire family, so that the family unit can again be exalted; however, it can also provide a spiritual focus for those who choose to embrace it on a personal level.

To me, the flame is a sacred symbol of life and faith, and of everything I hold dear. Vesta is a face in the flame, one that makes an impersonal universe feel a bit more personal. Her flame can quench the human longing to commune with the naturally divine, without having to buy into man-made doctrine that you just can't stomach.

It's a belief system with a big heart, too. In the Greco-Roman hierarchy of deities, the goddess Vesta was the granddaughter of Mother Nature herself.

Vestal spirituality advocates animal welfare and a deep respect for all life that walks, crawls and slithers upon the Earth, all life that swims in the waters and soars in the skies of our living planet. We don't live here alone.

By supporting humanist values and interests, New Vesta lights the way for social progress (i.e. same-sex marriage, the right to die with dignity) and scientific discovery that can illuminate how our home, the universe, really works.

This stands in contrast to the Dark Ages, that period of church-sanctioned scientific suppression that followed the banishment of Vesta.

In a world too-often plagued by violent religious intolerance, the New Vesta tradition is peaceful and humble. It co-exists with other belief and non-belief systems and opposes the religious indoctrination of children.

In the words of Kahlil Gibran, "Say not, 'I have found the truth,' but rather, 'I have found a truth.'" Vesta's flame offers a beautifully lit path to travel, but it is not the only path one can choose.

The Elysian Fields

Ah, the afterlife. It's a central theme in almost all religions for an obvious reason – death is scary as hell. It's depressing as hell, too. You mean I'll never again feel the warm embrace of my husband? Never again hear the sweet sound of my child's voice? Never again see my mother's loving smile? Never again.

It's been said that Edgar Allen Poe's poem *The Raven* is the most terrifying piece of literature ever written. "Quoth the raven, Nevermore." The "nevermore" means never again. It makes me want to cry just thinking about it.

I heard a lot of talk about heaven at the funeral. "He's in heaven now." "You will see him again in heaven." "Now he is with his parents in heaven." That kind of thing.

Just as we long for kind of comfort today, so too did Vesta's followers. They loved their husbands and children and parents as much as we do, and they felt the grief of their loss just as much as we do.

Vesta's faithful believed that after they died, they would reunite with lost loved ones in the Elysian Fields, a beautiful meadow filled with family, friends and eternal happiness.

The very idea of "paradise" and heaven is based on the Elysian Fields: a fertile field of vegetation, eternal spring, warm sun and joy. A place of renewal.

It was also a place of rebirth. Vesta's faithful were not obligated to believe they would spend eternity in the Elysian Fields, as appealing as that might be. They were free to follow their own spiritual instincts, and many believed in reincarnation: that their soul and the souls of their loved ones would be reborn again in the natural world to reunite in different forms.

After Alyssa's father's casket was lowered into the ground, I saw that this ancient belief in renewal and rebirth are still alive in modern funeral customs. The women in his family had prepared a bowl of wheat seeds and taken it to the cemetery: mourners each took a handful of these seeds and tossed them into the open grave to represent renewal and rebirth. From these seeds, the Elysian Fields would grow. From these seeds, life would spring anew.

The Eternal Flame

The Flamma Vesta may be eternal, but our time on this Earth is not. Yet our existence, however brief, becomes a note in the song of eternity. The eternal Flame of Vesta is a symbol of the universal energy from which each of us forms, like a spark flies out of out of a flame. Our lives, spirits and bodies are made of energy.

That is something Camilla tried to explain to me a long time ago, but now I think I know what it means.

Physics tells us that energy cannot be created or destroyed, and it is always changing form. So too are we. Our experiences and emotions, including the love we have for others, is part of that same energy that extends from the deepest reaches of space to the deepest reaches of the atoms that make up our bodies, the same energy that animates our lives and persists after our physical form breaks apart.

To me, Vesta's flame is a representation of that energy, both personal and universal. It is a symbol that asks me, every single day of my life, to choose to act in positive rather than negative ways. To use the energy that the universe has lent me as a force for good.

It reminds me to speak to the people in my life with patience and kindness, not criticism or contempt. It challenges me to offer an embrace, not a rejection. To show appreciation, not indifference. To break into spontaneous laughter, not erupt in anger. To adore and build up, not abandon or cut down. To pull toward, not push away.

I think that good things happen when we use our life's energy in this way. That's why it's important to find a symbolic, even elegant way to celebrate the way in which your life and energy intertwines with the lives and energies of those you love.

For a while, your energies exist together in this life. In time, and one by one, those energies will break apart and then unite again in whatever awaits us in the afterlife. Perhaps it is those green meadows of the Elysian Fields. When you look into a flame, you can see a flicker of this perpetuity. When you look deeper, you can see a flicker of your own soul.

To believe in Vesta is to believe in your family and in yourself. Her flame does not save families or lives by divine assistance, but rather by offering her light as inspiration. Use it as a way to channel your energy so that it makes your time on this earth better, and ensures that the energy you put back into the universe reflects the kind of eternity that you want to be part of.

The Power of Symbols

The wooden rosary that used to hang from the mirror on my grandmother's dresser. The black clothes the mourners wore and the crosses around their necks. The icon on the coffin. The colorful images on the stained glass windows. All religious symbols of faith, grief and reverence.

The Vesta tradition is steeped in such symbolism, starting with the sacred Flame of Vesta. The flame symbolizes the goddess herself. It also symbolizes family, energy, eternal life, purity, renewal and rebirth.

Offerings of mola salsa (loose salted flour or salted flour baked into small wafers) and libations of olive oil or wine represent a way to nourish and show gratitude for those things. The lararium symbolizes family devotion and love.

The Vestal candle that Camilla gave me was also rich in symbolism. White with heavy milk-glass folds of drapery, it symbolizes the robes and headdresses worn by the Vestal priestesses. It is round like the Temple of Vesta. The pure amber beeswax represents the purity of the goddess and her priestesses, as well as the purity of creation itself.

The day that I met Camilla was symbolic, too. The first day of March, a traditional day of renewal and rediscovery. Of fresh starts. Of choosing between those two wolves that are symbolic of the struggle within all of us, and that represent the wisdom and strength within all of us.

I've always loved symbols, especially religious symbols, yet I used to think that people who surrounded themselves with such symbols were kind of simple-minded. You need to wear a cross around your neck to feel religious? You need to hold a rosary to pray? You need to look at that icon to see the face of your god? Their reliance on symbols seemed like a weakness.

Now I know it's a strength. Surrounding yourself with the symbols of your spirituality makes you stronger. This is why the Flamma Vesta burns in my furnace and my house feels warmer than before: maybe it's just my imagination, but it sure feels that way.

This is why Vestal candles can be found in each room of my home. This is why our family lararium is packed with mementoes of the people I love, and why beautiful pictures of Vesta's temple adorn my walls.

Now, I see symbolism everywhere. In Vancouver, Don and I stayed in a boutique hotel on the Vancouver waterfront. After we parked and walked toward the entrance, I couldn't help but laugh out loud. An eternal flame was burning just outside the main entrance of the hotel. To me, of course, this fire was the Flame of Vesta.

After we put our bags in our room, we strolled along the pier until we stumbled upon a small, round grassy space enclosed on all sides by a circle of trees. In the earliest days of Vesta worship, the temple was likely a round enclosure similar to this, with trees serving as natural columns. To me, of course, this little space was an organic Temple of Vesta.

I've gone from one extreme to the other: from laughing at those who found meaning in such random sights and happenings, to looking for such meaning in what might otherwise seem like empty coincidence.

Just as I chose to find happiness in my life, I have chosen to find meaning in it, too. And to be honest, I like my new way of looking at life a lot better. It adds depth and dimension, even a sense of destiny, to my life. It connects my past, present and future so that I feel a sense of spiritual constancy as I go through my days.

When we finally arrived back home from the funeral, a gift was waiting for me in the mail. Don had ordered it a couple weeks earlier: a tiny meteorite fragment from the Vesta asteroid. I immediately had it made into a pendant that I could wear around my neck as my personal symbol of Vestal spirituality.

It is a symbol that is rich in meaning to me. Not only does it represent Vesta by carrying her name, it also reminds me of the countless hours that my husband, son and I have spent stargazing as a family.

It reminds me of Camilla, too. The pendant around my neck contains a sliver of the very asteroid that was seen so brightly in the night sky in 1989, the same year that she came into my life and introduced me to the first flickers of faith.

Don had done quite a bit of research into meteorites to snag this cosmic gem, and it turns out that it too had a story to tell. It is a fragment of the so-called Johnstown meteorite – apparently quite famous in meteorite collector circles – which struck the Earth on July 6, 1924 outside a church where, of all things, a funeral service was being held.

The funny part is, Don had researched and ordered this meteorite a week before my friend's dad passed away, before we knew that we'd soon be attending a funeral. Years ago, I'd dismiss this as coincidence. Now I'm not so sure.

CHAPTER X

Spiritual Evolution

It is not the strongest of the species that survives, nor the most intelligent that survives. It is the one that is the most adaptable to change.
- Charles Darwin, English Biologist, 1809 – 1882 CE

Love in its essence is spiritual fire.
- Seneca the Younger, Roman Philosopher, 4 BCE – 65 CE

    I'm an evolutionist. I believe in the principles of biological evolution – that adaptation leads to survival. That gradual growth and development are natural, necessary and desirable.
    When Charles Darwin left England for the Galapagos Islands in the early 1800's, he still believed in Biblical creationism; however, his beliefs evolved over time as the evidence for biological evolution became undeniable.

What made him change his mind? Finch beaks. Cute little chirping finch beaks. A short beak here, a long beak there, a perfect beak everywhere.

Now I believe in spiritual evolution, too. As I learned to embrace the New Vesta tradition, to figure out what it all meant and how it fit in my world, I often felt like I was standing on my own little Galapagos Island where my ideas about religion, spirituality and meaning were evolving and adapting to help me survive an ever-changing life.

I evolved from a focus on career and control to a focus on family and friendship. From criticism and self-importance to gratitude and humility. From never-enough to fulfillment. From cynicism to acceptance. From darkness to light.

By evolving, by adapting, my spirit has survived. So too has my marriage, my family and my happiness. I don't have anything tangible, like finch beaks, to prove that spiritual evolution exists. I just have my own experience and belief. Yet these too can be measured. Not in inches, but in the ways they have changed my life for the better.

The Vesta tradition has also evolved, and over a much longer timeline. As a spirituality that began as fire worship, the spark of Vesta was lit when Homo erectus learned to control fire almost a million years ago, or perhaps even earlier, during the Stone Age some 2.5 million years ago, when our ancestor hominids marveled at the mystery of fire.

Fire worship is one of the earliest forms of "religion" known to humankind. There is something instinctual about the way humans revere fire, as we if know it is fundamental to our existence. If you've ever lost yourself staring into a fire or flame, you've felt it. It has a living presence that gives us our most elemental religious experience.

But just over a hundred years ago, families started flipping switches instead of lighting candles. Electricity and lightbulbs took the place of candles and flame and the magic was lost. What we gained in convenience and effectiveness, we lost in warmth and sacredness.

Fire worship was personified in the form of the goddess Vesta as far back as the Bronze Age, when she was known by her Greek name of Hestia. It was the Romans, however, that perceived her in a far more personal and prevalent way, and who worshipped her flame both in their homes and in her temple, around which grew and evolved the great Roman Empire.

The New Vesta tradition continues to evolve into a spirituality that is as relevant in the modern world as it was in antiquity. Despite the years and the changing world and the adaptations it has had to make, it has survived.

More than that, it is once again starting to thrive. I can't keep my Vestal candles in stock, and have had to start distributing wooden wicks – pre-lit with the Flamma Vesta – to women who wish to add a spark of sacredness to their homes.

Life's Main Intersection

When I first met Vesta in Rome, life was just beginning to give me things. A post-secondary education, a professional career, the interests and personality that would define me, life-long friends, a husband, a child and my own family. Life just kept giving and giving.

When I met Vesta for the second time, in Las Vegas, life was at that pivotal intersection – let's call it middle-age – where it begins to slow and, ever so gradually, begin to take things away. I was losing my youth, my parents were getting older, my son was starting to grow up, and my marriage was beginning to become complacent. I was starting to lose interest in life. What else was left to do? What else was left to acquire or discover?

It's easy to sit at that intersection, spinning your wheels in neutral, doing nothing but staring in the rearview mirror in sadness or regret for days gone by. It's easy to become apathetic, bitter or just plain bored with life, especially as the years continue to fly by. It's hard to get enough traction to start moving again. Where does one get the momentum?

For me, the momentum came from faith. It came from realizing that my long-ago meeting with Camilla was inescapably and intimately destined to link my past with my present. It was like a long, twisting vine of laurel that wound its way through all the days of my life, just as the laurel vines once wound around the Temple of Vesta.

As a formerly non-spiritual person, that realization fascinated me. It re-ignited my interest in life. And not just in my life – that seems so arrogant and self-indulgent – but in all life. In the wonder of life itself.

I realized that life isn't random or temporary or inconsequential. It isn't just about cosmic explosions and DNA and adaptive biology. I realized that it's okay to feel that there's more to life than can be seen through a microscope or a telescope.

I think we can get out of that lifeless, dead-end intersection by making a choice. A choice to keep moving and to be fascinated by life, even when – perhaps especially when – the fascination is starting to wear off.

Sparks and Superpowers

What do we do when a fire has gone out? We add a spark and get it going again. It's the same thing with life. If you've lost your happiness or your fascination, you need to re-ignite those. That starts with having an open mind and a curious nature.

Open-mindedness and curiosity can lead you down some unexpected paths, perhaps even paths that you formerly refused to explore. I, for example, now know more about superheroes than any other middle-aged woman on Earth. But I never used to like superheroes. Okay, there was always something a little charming about Superman and those baby blues, but that was it.

Then along came my son. He didn't like superheroes the way that other kids like superheroes. It wasn't just, "Spiderman is cool" or "Batman's awesome." He was an true expert in superhero comics and immersed himself in the culture.

His fascination came out of nowhere. Neither me, Don nor anyone in our family had ever been overly interested in this genre, but for whatever reason our kid was utterly obsessed with it from the moment he first saw a cape flap in the wind.

He would go on and on about alternate dimensions, which comic editions were the most rare or valuable, which artist and writers were the best, who were the most vile archenemies, what origin stories were the most dramatic, which story arcs he agreed or disagreed with and which actors were cast properly in movie adaptations.

To be honest, it sometimes bored the life out of me. I found myself tuning out and sometimes turning away from him.

But then I forced myself to have an open mind and to be curious about superheroes, if only out of parental obligation. Don and I took him to comic conventions where he'd engage in the most intense conversations with complete strangers about vintage Marvel or DC comics and how Hawkeye vs. the U.S. Agent in Avenger's West Coast was a good one, and where at ten-years-old he could masterfully negotiate a $70.00 vintage comic book down to $30.00.

I shamelessly exploited my media connections so that he could speak with comic book and sci-fi legends from Stan Lee to Carrie Fisher. He would bring different costumes – a Jawa, Captain America, Cad Bane – and we couldn't take more than ten steps without someone snapping his picture.

And you know what? Now I like superheroes. Now I like comic conventions. They're escapist and ridiculous and fun as hell. I adapted to and embraced my son's interest, even though it held no appeal for me at first, and it turned out to become a fundamental part of the way that I bond with my child. That was how a spark became a kind of superpower.

Make the choice to evolve by adapting to your life. Adapt and you will continue to experience the wonder of existence. Adapt and you will continue to find new things that fascinate you. Adapt and you will find the spark that re-ignites your happiness.

Adapt to your life as it changes, just as the flame adapts when the wood shifts in the hearth. If it didn't, its fire would go out.

Sparks and Secrets

The New Vesta secret is multifaceted. There is the secret that Camilla passed down to me at the ruins of the Temple of Vesta in the Roman Forum: that she and the faithful Vestals before her had kept the sacred flame burning in secret throughout the generations, sometimes at great risk to themselves. We owe these brave, remarkable women so much.

There is also the secret that burns deep within the Immaculate Heart of the Virgin Mary: that her "flame of love" is actually the Flame of Vesta. So much of Mary, that beloved religious figure, is based on a goddess who was equally beloved in her time, who has continued to be worshipped by some, and who is once again illuminating homes and lives with her tradition.

But perhaps the greatest secrets of all are the ones that we discover ourselves when we look into the sacred Flamma Vesta. When we fall into silent reflection and reverence for her eternal flame. The secret to unlocking the potential of our own woman's and self-intuition. The secret to our own faith and happiness. The secret to our own enduring fascination with life.

It is a choice to have faith and to be happy. It is a choice to remain fascinated by our time on this Earth. Life is BIG. We can too easily forget that when our minds and hearts shrink with age or disillusionment, or when life simply doesn't live up to the expectations we once forced upon it. Ultimately, my newfound faith has been as much a spiritual choice as a spiritual awakening.

I am finishing this book in the dead of winter. In fact, it's one of the coldest and snowiest winters on record. You wouldn't know it from our home, though. The Flamma Vesta warms and lights our household just as it warmed and lit the households of thousands of other families over many centuries.

Yet even in the darkness of winter, the spark of spring endures and expands. My family and I are planning a vacation to Rome so that we can all visit the Temple of Vesta together. We will go in March and renew the flame in the same spot that Camilla renewed it so many years ago. To quote the ancient writer Ovid, "the renewed flame gains strength." I've already seen how true that is.

Before we go to Italy, however, we are stopping to visit Alyssa's family in Greece. We became fast friends with them while attending her dad's funeral and, when I told them about my experience with Vesta, they looked at me with blanched faces.

Only weeks before the funeral, they had hired a contractor to rip out an ancient stone hearth from an old house they own on the Island of Crete – and believe me, an "old house" in Greece is indeed an old house. After looking at the fireplace, the contractor walked out of the house, shaking his head. "The spirit of Hestia is there," he said. "I will not destroy it. Find someone else if you want it out."

And so the fireplace was restored, not removed. It's that house that my family and I will be staying in and it makes me wonder: Will I too feel the spirit of Vesta there? When we light the fire, will I sense the memories and experiences of the many families – grandparents, mothers, fathers, children and favorite pets – who for generations sat, ate, talked, played and loved each other in front of Vesta's fire?

What will it be like to visit the Temple of Ve___ many years and changes? Will I once again hear the ___ cats asking for a bit of salami or see shadows of long ___ priestesses glide over the stone pillars?

Will the Flame of Vesta once again cast its s___ ___ columns? I don't know. Perhaps I will be just as happy to see the shadow of Superman move across the great white columns as my son flies an action figure in the Italian sunshine.

Whenever I light the Flamma Vesta in my home, whether it's in a candle or in our family fireplace, a profound sense of sacredness fills the space around me. It should, since the presence of Vesta's flame makes the home a more sacred space than any church, synagogue or temple.

I see Vesta's face in the flame, hear her voice in the crackle of the wood and feel her energy flow out of her fire and into my life. It is a spiritual experience each and every time, one that grounds me and lifts me up in the selfsame moment.

With each flicker of her flame, I feel reverence for my life and a sort of awe-inspiring comfort for what lies beyond it. With each snap of the wood, I hear Vesta reminding me to love my husband and son with all my energy, and then promising me that that love and energy will someday return to become part of the universal energy that moves us all from here to eternity.

I wonder what happened to Camilla. How long did she live? Where are the sons that she spoke of? I wonder, too, what she would think of me. I hope she would be proud but, even more than that, I hope she would find peace knowing that, despite my many flaws, I am devoted to keeping her beloved faith and flame alight in my own life, in my own way.

There are still so many things to wonder about in this life. There are still so many secrets to know about ourselves. With nothing more than a spark and a little flame to see by, you can seek out those secrets.

What makes you curious? What makes you laugh? What fascinates you or fills you with faith? What feels sacred to you? What regrets might you have on your deathbed and what are you doing, today, to change that? What choices will you make in your life?

Those are important questions. Those are the kinds of questions a person can only answer when she chooses to fully and gracefully participate in the changing phases of her life, knowing that each chapter is part of a never-ending narrative.

I hope you will light a candle, focus on the flame, and discover those answers within yourself. That is how to renew a life.

After all, the greatest discoveries – the ones that can help you find faith and happiness – aren't waiting for you at the top of the career ladder or in an exotic foreign country. They aren't waiting for you at the summit of a remote mystical mountain, under the gold-gilded dome of a great marble cathedral, or even in the ruins of an ancient temple.

They're waiting for you at home.

SUPPLEMENT

The Five Tenets of the New Vesta Tradition

While I hope my story will inspire you to revere your family life and find happiness at home – after all, that is the spirit of Vesta – there may be some readers who wish to incorporate certain aspects of this faith in their home life in a more practical way.

For that reason, I've included in this supplement the five most common tenets that are practiced by today's New Vesta followers. You will have read about each of these tenets in this book, so they will be somewhat familiar to you.

Tenet #1 of the New Vesta Tradition:
A Household Lararium with Vestal Candle

A lararium or family altar can be located wherever you wish; however, the entrance or foyer to your home holds the most significant meaning, as it oversees the comings and goings of family members from the home.

A lararium altar can be modest, even as simple as a shelf, cabinet or table top. It can also be more elaborate and take the shape of a rounded or traditional Greco-Roman temple. It may or may not have doors. A lararium with one or two front doors, hinged to open and close, can preserve the privacy of the family's place of worship.

This altar can be classical or modern, home-made or manufactured. Some women may prefer the lararium to stand out from the rest of the home's décor, while others may prefer that it blend into the home's furnishings and fashion.

A candle that symbolizes the Flamma Vesta should be placed in the center of the lararium. A statue of the goddess Vesta may also adorn the lararium, although this is not necessary. A reproduction of the Temple of Vesta or an image of it (i.e. a photograph of the ruins or a reconstructed drawing of the complete temple) is a wonderful way to pay tribute.

Because the Temple of Vesta was traditionally adorned with laurels, you may also wish to decorate your lararium – especially during special family occasions – with laurel leaves strung into wreaths or garland or even sprinkled over the altar. You can grow a laurel tree or bush in your yard for this purpose. A simpler option is to grow an indoor herb garden that contains a bay herb: plant this in a small Roman-style pot, place it on your lararium, and you have year-round laurel adornment for your family altar.

Be sure to create a lararium that you love and that reflects your style, flair and personality. It should make you happy whenever you look at it, and should remind you of the things that are most important to you. Other than the one constant – the presence of a Flamma Vesta candle in the center – use your own fashion sense and have some fun with it.

Whether it is created on a wooden cabinet, glass table or even a wine cart, the lararium is your personal altar to Vesta. It is a reminder to revere your home and those you are fortunate enough to share it with.

Tenet #2 of the New Vesta Tradition: Daily Offerings and Prayer

Offerings to Vesta should be made at the beginning and end of each meal. The traditional Vestal offering, prepared by the Vestal priestesses, was called mola salsa. A simple version of mola salsa can be made by combining coarse-ground flour and salt in a bowl. A bit of this loose mixture can be sprinkled into the flame of your Vestal candle.

You can also make mola salsa wafers or cake by combining flour, salt and a small amount of water together, lightly kneading the dough mixture and then flattening and shaping it into small, thin, round wafers. Place the wafers on a floured baking sheet and either let them harden or put them in a pre-heated oven and bake them for a few minutes. The wafer can be broken apart and its crumbs sprinkled into the sacred flame, or the intact wafer can simply be passed over the flame, thus preventing debris from collecting in the candle wax.

Because mola salsa is a salt-purified offering, it is quite salty in taste; however, you can bake or purchase regular flatbread which can be crumbled and sprinkled into the sacred flame, or passed over the flame, before it is eaten by the family.

Sweeter offerings can be made, such as fine pastry crumbs.

A libation of olive oil or wine can be given. Pour the liquid into a shallow bowl: this heralds back to the ancient patera or libation bowl that the Vestal priestesses used. Dip your fingers into the oil or wine and sprinkle it into the sacred flame.

Mealtime prayers to Vesta may accompany these offerings. Prayers to Vesta need not be elaborate or formal. She was a modest goddess, moved more by authenticity than affected adoration.

Simple prayers may include:

Vesta, please enter this home and accept our modest offering. Light our family's way, together and separately, as we honor our lives and our home.

Vesta, kindly come and dwell in our home in friendship. Accept our offering. Protect we who live here and remind us to revere this home, the object of our shared devotion.

Vesta, who dwells in the sacred and eternal fire, enter this home where we dwell in love and friendship. Let us see your face in our flame and hear your laughter in our fire. Accept our offering and gratitude for your devotion to our home.

Prayers may be made for the health and happiness of the family as a whole, or for individual family members or friends who may need extra support. Prayers should not be protracted or beseeching, but rather brief and respectful.

In addition to mealtime worship, an end-of-day candle ritual can also be performed. When the last person to arrive home at the end of the day comes through the door, she or he can light the Vestal candle and say a brief prayer of gratitude that the family is safe and together.

This ritual can be done in reverse, too – the candle can continue to burn until the last family member arrives home and extinguishes the flame for the night, thus symbolizing that the family is all under one roof. This ritual may also include an offering of mola salsa, oil or wine.

Tenet #3 of the New Vesta Tradition: Ancestral Roots

Mementoes of respected family members, living and dead, should be placed on the lararium. These can be photographs, carvings or trinkets that remind you of them. A family tree should be done and shared with family members. If you cannot gather enough information from relatives to build a family tree, there are online ancestry and heritage services that can help.

Living grandparents or great-grandparents can be invited to gift something of meaning to the family lararium, and should be invited to share stories about their struggles and successes in life. They may be able to provide more information about your, and their, distant ancestors. They should also be consulted for their advice and thoughts, which should always be received with appreciation and gratitude, especially by any children in the home.

Placing a small statue or figure of a tree on your household lararium can also serve as a visual reminder that your family has deep ancestral roots that support its many branches. As with everything on your family altar, this should be unique to your style.

Some women may wish to purchase a many-branched tree statue and, depending on your taste and the tree's design, hang small family photos or mementoes from the branches. Others may wish to fashion a tree out of branches collected from their own yard or a family trip to the park. Those with a crafty streak may wish to create a tree out of clay or other materials, perhaps asking their children to help design and paint it.

Tenet #4 (Part 1) of the New Vesta Tradition: Light Reflection

(Note: This candlelit practice has two parts: the first is a daily ritual presented here, while the second is a periodic ritual presented next.)

Light reflection is a daily ritual of focusing on the Flamma Vesta. Its purpose is to reflect upon the good things in your life to create sparks of positive thoughts, emotions and behaviors. Its purpose is also to tap into your woman's intuition if you need answers to life's questions.

This ritual should be performed in a quiet room that can be made completely dark. You should be able to sit comfortably in this space, whether in a chair or on a floor cushion. You should also have a table or other surface upon which to burn your Vestal candle.

Enter this room and light the Vestal candle. Turn off the lights and sit in front of the candle. Look into the flame. Watch its movements, study its color, enjoy its glow. Listen to the flame. Hear it crackle as it burns the wooden wick. Focus on these sensory inputs – the sight and sound of Vesta's sacred, eternal flame – and push every other sight, sound, scent, taste and feeling from your mind and body.

As you stare into the light of the Flamma Vesta, reflect upon what makes you happy. People, places, hopes. Reflect upon what is good about your life. Your family, friends, job, interests or passions. Reflect upon what brings laughter and joy to your life.

If you are struggling with a particular problem, whether a relationship issue or a health issue, reflect upon what is good about that situation.

For example, you might reflect upon the kind things your partner has said or done for you in the past, or how much better you feel after you have exercised, eaten well or broken a bad health habit. There is good in almost any situation. Find it and focus on it. You can also ask yourself a direct question and focus on the flame as you "intuit" the answer.

This ritual should be performed twice a day – morning and evening – so that you can focus your first and last thoughts and emotions of the day into happy, affirming and positive ones. It should take approximately five to ten minutes.

If you wish, you may make a mola salsa or olive oil offering to Vesta before you extinguish the flame, although this is not necessary.

Beginning your day with this kind of light reflection and Vestal focus can profoundly affect how your day is going to play out. It can influence the way you speak to and treat others, the way you carry yourself, the way you react to unexpected or unpleasant events, the way you feel and the way others feel about you. Its effects can last all day long.

Ending your day with this Vestal ritual hits the refresh button and reminds you to embrace the evening with joy, gratitude and affection for those in your life. It ensures that the last words on your lips at night express love and kindness.

The simplicity of this ritual is deceptive. Don't be fooled. It offers one of the most powerful ways for the spirit of Vesta to add a positive spark of energy to your life and to light your way, every day and every night. It's far too easy for the clouds of negativity to darken our thoughts, emotions and behaviors. The light of Vesta can help us (and by extension our families) live under sunnier skies, day in and day out.

If you wish to commune with Vesta, you can pray – silently or aloud – to her during this ritual. Converse with her, as you would a trusted friend, about your worries and she will help you shoulder their weight. Share your joy with her, and it will grow even greater.

Tenet #4 (Part 2) of the New Vesta Tradition: Light Reflection & Renewal

(Note: This candlelit practice has two parts: the first is a daily ritual presented previously, while the second is a periodic ritual presented here.)

If you long for a new beginning in your life, the following Vestal cleansing and renewing ritual can help you achieve it, both symbolically and practically. Perform it whenever you feel the need for a fresh start or are having trouble moving forward in your life.

This ritual should be done in the same dark, quiet room in which you practice light reflection, since it is a cathartic extension of that daily ritual; however, this ritual requires that you have a pen and two sheets of paper, as well as a surface to write upon.

You will also need just enough light to write by: if your Vestal candle isn't bright enough, find a heavily shaded lamp or soft-light bulb to write by, as these will not hurt your eyes when turned on.

To begin, sit in the darkened room with only the sight and sound of the Flamma Vesta before you. Slowly picture in your mind a wildfire raging through an old forest. It burns and crackles and consumes half-dead trees, rotting wood and the pestilence that has been plaguing the forest for years and preventing it from flourishing like it used it, or perhaps never had the chance to. The fire rages for days. Plumes of black smoke rise to fill the air. The heat and the sound are overpowering.

But then it all starts to subside. The fire dies down and a warm mist of rain descends upon the ashes, cooling them. Out of the sterile silence, a few birds start to sing. And then through the black-charred pillars of the few trees still standing, you see two wolves. One is black and one is white. They are both looking at you with their grey eyes, grey like the ashes, and they're running toward you, fast and determined as though on the hunt.

You know you can't run. If you do, they'll only pursue and there's no way you can outrun them. So you stand and wait as they race toward you with their grey eyes and their breath that mixes with the mist of the rain. You stand and wait as the sound of their heavy breath, the pounding of their paws on the scorched forest floor, reverberates around you and closes in.

They run, fast and hard, until they are so close you expect to feel their weight knock you over and their sharp white teeth sink into your neck. But instead they stop abruptly at your feet, causing clouds of ash to swirl around your head. They look up at you, panting and expectant. You can feel their hot breath on your legs. You can hear the deep growl in their throats. But they don't move, don't attack. They're waiting for something. But for what?

They're waiting to see which one of them you will feed.

And you will feed one of them. Not with meat, but with words that you will speak aloud.

But first, you will silently write each of them a letter.

If necessary, turn on the soft light in your room and gather your writing supplies.

On one sheet of paper, write to the black wolf about all the things in your life that make you angry, jealous, regretful, hateful, unhappy, resentful, egocentric, self-pitying or self-doubting. You can write about who hurt you as a child or as an adult. About those you miss. About how you feel lost or have doubts. About the mistakes you have made. You can write about unrequited love, spouses who betrayed you, personal or financial failures, parents or partners who let you down.

Write to the wolf and tell him how these feelings affect your life and your relationships. How they scare you, sadden you or hold you back.

On the other sheet of paper, write to the white wolf about all the things in your life that make you serene, grateful, full of perspective, loving, joyful, empathetic, kind, make you laugh or give you conviction. You can write about who has been kind to you. About your family and friendships and those who love you. About the good decisions you have made, what you cherish and how strong you can be. About your dreams for the future.

Write to the wolf and tell him how these feelings affect your life and your relationships. How they fill you with hope and energy, and push you forward.

Now decide which wolf you are going to feed.

Burn the letter to the wolf you want to starve, letting the paper disintegrate in the cleansing flame of your Vestal candle. As the paper disappears, so too does the hurt on it.

Gather the ashes. Bury them in the ground or release them in the wind. It doesn't matter.

Now feed the wolf you want to survive: that is, the white wolf. Read your letter – the one about joy and hope and gratitude – aloud to him, in front of the Flame of Vesta. Let him feast on your words and watch him grow stronger, faster and wiser than the other wolf.

Read the letter to him as many times as you like and then store it away in a secret place so that whenever he needs nourishment, you can take it out and read it to him again.

This ritual can be done on an as-needed basis, whenever you find yourself struggling with negative thoughts, memories or emotions that are holding you back. It should also be performed on a yearly basis, every March 1st, the traditional date of Vestal renewal.

Tenet #5 of the New Vesta Tradition: Wearing a Vestal Symbol

A Vestal symbol isn't just a way to show your faith: it is also a way to feel the presence and power of New Vesta in your life on a daily basis.

I wear a pendant made from a sliver of the meteorite Vesta. This has personal meaning and symbolism to me in a number of ways. Followers of New Vesta should choose symbols that have meaning to them, and that reflect their unique life experiences.

Jewelry is a common way to wear a Vestal symbol. You can wear a simple pendant or charm with either the letter "V" or a flame to represent Vesta or the Flamma Vesta. These are the most customary Vestal symbols.

You can also have a jeweler melt down an old piece of jewelry, whether from a bitter ex-partner or a beloved relative, and remodel it into a Vestal symbol. This renewal process can be cathartic. Choose a customary Vestal symbol or, if you wish, a unique design that speaks to you. If you're a stargazer like me, for example, you might choose the planetary symbol of the Vesta 4 asteroid, which represents the altar of Vesta with its sacred fire: ⚶.

Certain gems and precious stones can also symbolize the Flame of Vesta. A fire opal is a natural gemstone that contains light-reflecting hues of color in red, orange, yellow and magenta. When worn as a pendant or charm, it reflects a spark of the Flamma Vesta.

Dragon's Breath is a man-made glass stone, often set in sterling silver, that is made to resemble a fire opal. It is made by adding flecks of metal into molten glass. This results in vibrant, lovely flashes of "fire" inside the glass. Dragon's Breath jewelry may be of particular interest to Vesta faithful as it is an affordable yet collectible stone, one that is available in a variety of hues, shapes and settings.

A white pearl necklace, bracelet or pair of earrings can symbolize the purity of Vesta, as well as the white marble of the Temple of Vesta and the white robes of the Vestal priestesses. In the same way, white clothing and fashion accessories can be worn as Vestal symbols. Wearing a white sweater, scarf or belt, or even carrying a white handbag, can incorporate the New Vesta tradition into your day to day life.

Original and low-cost reproduction ancient Roman coins are available from collectors and retailers, many of whom sell online: choose a coin that has an image of Vesta and/or the Temple of Vesta. You can have a jeweler set the coin into a ring of metal or gold so that you can wear it as a necklace or charm. Alternatively, many sellers have already framed these coins (whether authentic or copies) into pendants, some of which boast gemstones and unique design.

Finally, original and affordable faux ancient Roman jewelry of the type popularly worn by women during the time when Vesta was most openly worshipped is also available from collectors and retailers, including online ones. Wearing antique rings, pendants, bracelets, brooches and glass beads is a meaningful way to present yourself as an adherent of the New Vesta spiritual tradition, and to bring the goddess's Old World presence into the New World.

The power of Vesta extends over altars and hearths, and thus all prayers and all offerings end with the goddess, because she is the guardian of the innermost things.

- Cicero, *De Natura Deorum*

For more information on the New Vesta tradition, or to request a Vestal candle or pre-lit Vestal wick to burn the authentic Flame of Vesta in your own home, visit **NewVesta.com**.

Look for more books on the New Vesta tradition, including *The New Vesta Home: How a Renewed Tradition Can Keep Your Marriage & Family Together.*

All best, in Vesta.

Made in the USA
San Bernardino, CA
19 January 2016